Outcomes

This book is to be returned on or before
the last date stamped below.

Outcomes:
NVQs and the Emerging Model of Education and Training

by

Gilbert Jessup

 The Falmer Press

(A member of the Taylor & Franics Group)
London · New York · Philadelphia

UK   The Falmer Press, 4 John St, London WC1N 2ET
USA   The Falmer Press, Taylor & Francis Inc., 1900 Frost Road, Suite 101,
       Bristol, PA 19007

© Gilbert Jessup 1991

First published 1991   Reprinted 1991, 1994

British Library Cataloguing in Publication Data
Jessup, Gilbert
    Outcomes: NVQs and the emerging model of education and training.
    1. Great Britain. Further education institutions.
    Vocational courses
    I. Title
    374.0130941

    ISBN 1–85000–972–4
    ISBN 1–85000–973–2 (pbk.)

Library of Congress Cataloging-in-Publication Data
Jessup, Gilbert.
    Outcomes: NVQs and the emerging model of education and train-
ing/Gilbert Jessup.
        p.   cm.
    Includes bibliographical references and index.
    ISBN 1–85000–972–4   ISBN 1–85000–973–2 (pbk.):
    1. Vocational education—Great Britain.   2. Vocational qualifications
—Great Britain.   I. Title.
LC1047.G7J37   1991
370.11'3'0941—dc20   91–48315
                                                                  CIP

Jacket design by Caroline Archer

Typeset in 10/12 pt Bembo by
Graphicraft Typesetters Ltd., Hong Kong.

Printed in Great Britain by Burgess Science Press, Basingstoke on paper
which has a specified pH value on final paper manufacture of not less
than 7.5 and is therefore 'acid free'.

Contents

Contents

Part Three: Outstanding Issues

Appendices

Foreword

This is an important book.

It is important for two reasons: (1) it meets a need and (2), it provides an authoritative, personal perspective on the thinking behind the emerging model of education and training.

National Vocational Qualifications (NVQs) have already touched the lives of millions of people in Britain (the millionth National Record (NROVA) was issued earlier this year); there was an urgent need for an informed and authoritative explanation of the many different facets of NVQs: who they are for, why they have been developed, how they work, the benefits they confer. Gilbert Jessup provides that explanation very lucidly, but he goes much further: he draws together strands from many different developments to explain how NVQs relate coherently to a wide range of issues in education and training.

Gilbert Jessup, is Director of Research, Development and Information at the NCVQ. Although this book is a personal statement and does not necessarily reflect NCVQ policy, its publication marks a subtle but significant shift in emphasis, signalled by the title. The emphasis is on outcomes, the focus on education and training, not, significantly, vocational education and training. This allows him scope to broach all outcomes (not exclusively 'competency-based') and all education and training. A focus on the outcomes of learning is listed as the second fundamental criterion underlying NVQs but Gilbert Jessup sees it as the key concept in the emerging competency-based model because it confers a vital principle of coherence on all the activities which characterize the NVQ approach, most notably:

A genuinely comprehensive Framework, where individual qualifications (and even 'part qualifications') relate to each other;

Open access and progression;

The accreditation of prior learning;

Independence of mode of learning, or attendance;

A 'demystified' assessment process which is open, and equitable and 'fit for purpose'.

These are not just desirable characteristics, they can be shown to follow logically and coherently from the adoption of 'outcomes' as the organizing principle. For the first time in the history of education and training in this country, it is becoming possible to plot the contribution and the relationship between different kinds of qualification.

The structure of degree programmes and their nomenclature in British universities is extremely complex but ultimately comprehensible to anyone prepared to take the time to get to know the 'system' this contrasts starkly with the provision of vocational and professional qualifications, which have been frequently likened to a 'jungle'. Last year, for instance, some two million qualifications were awarded by over three hundred different awarding bodies. These awarding bodies, which largely derive their income from examination fees, are frequently in sourdine competition with each other, and have, historically, largely ignored or declined to recognise each other's awards. It has thus been impossible for any individual fully to comprehend the 'system' and to plan knowledgeably for progression. With the creation of the NCVQ Database, Gilbert Jessup demonstrates it will be possible for anyone with access to a terminal to interrogate any of the qualifications within the framework and to make the best use of provision in terms of his or her needs, his or her career goals.

Gilbert Jessup recognizes that in promoting competence, there may be other legitimate and worthwhile objectives other than competency:

> In many areas, particularly at the higher levels of competence, there is a related body of knowledge and theory which underpins a wide range of competent performance. This body of knowledge would normally have its own internal coherence and should be acquired and understood by students. It would not be appropriate to perceive it, and assess it, simply, in relation to elements of competence (p. 125).

Indeed, the development of generic competences or core skills (cf. p. 80) which contribute to competency but are not themselves competences further attests the wider interest in targeted outcomes.

The important point for Gilbert Jessup is that education and training should be goal-directed towards explicit outcomes, although, again, he is quick to assert that predetermined outcomes are not necessarily the only worthwhile outcomes:

> Whether pursuing general or specific objectives individuals will learn more effectively if they are clear about the targets or learning out-

comes they are trying to achieve. Learning is a purposive activity and should be targeted on explicit outcomes. This should not discourage incidental and additional learning taking place en route which is not part of the plan. Nor should it stop people following tangential lines of enquiry out of curiosity. In fact, such additional learning is more likely to be stimulated within the context of a learning plan (p. 5).

This argument is set in a context where the actual outcomes of learning may be negligible or even counterproductive; he emphasizes this by distinguishing aims and objectives from outcomes:

> . . . the way Shakespeare or poetry are taught in schools may actually put more people off these pursuits as adults than the number it stimulates to continue. This is not to question the aim of such education, only the outcome (p. 5).

It is important to appreciate that the model in the title is, indeed, an emerging model, and nothing is set in tablets of stone. Although the primary purpose of this book is to provide a much needed comprehensive account of the thinking behind NVQs and therefore to inform, there is another purpose. That purpose is to stimulate interest and informed debate, so that the process can be carried forward and enhanced by the experience and perspectives of a wider public with an interest in this important area of development.

I said earlier that this was a 'personal statement'; what may not be apparent from reading the text is the extent to which Gilbert Jessup's personal contribution has shaped so many developments in the emerging model of education and training which is the subject of this book.

An internal paper, first drafted in 1984 before the NCVQ was conceived when he was at the MSC (see Appendix A) provides a blueprint for subsequent developments. The recognition that 'function' is a more embracing and relevant concept than 'task' lay in the future. In all other respects, this paper exhibits a remarkable foresight, presaging virtually every important advance in the competence based movement.

In particular, Gilbert Jessup grasped the fundamental significance of 'standards of a new kind', one idea buried among many other ideas, in the White Paper 'New Training Initiative' and focused on this as the guiding principle for future provision.

Many of the documents and papers to which he refers, as 'MSC' or 'NCVQ' were in fact written by him; many of the initiatives described were of his making, many of the research projects were directed or devised by him; and even where other researchers are rightly attributed as authors, he has made salient contributions, often directly, often as a member of a committee or steering group. His stance may be refreshingly reticent and even modest; his personal achievement certainly is not.

Throughout the book, Gilbert Jessup argues cogently that only the learner should seek to control learning; this book may be seen as a valuable contribution to that process.

Dr. John Burke,
Senior Fellow,
Institute of Continuing and Professional Education
University of Sussex.

Preface

Since completing this book two months ago the national debate on education and training has risen to new heights. The Labour Party has made education its 'top priority' and the Prime Minister has said it will be 'at the heart of the debate' in the next election. A recent House of Lords' report suggests legislation is needed to ensure training is provided for all 16 to 18 year-olds not in full-time education. Others suggest financial incentives. Standards are said to be falling or rising depending on the measures taken, but all agree that they are not high enough.

Irrespective of legislation and funding, we require a more coherent system in which to organise education and training to ensure we get value for money from our investment. We also need to ensure that the system is tailored to meet the needs of individuals.

This book starts by looking at the process of individual learning and considers how we can make learning more relevant and available to people of all ages and all abilities. It looks particularly at the introduction of National Vocational Qualifications and the National Curriculum, the models on which they are based and their implications. It goes further to indicate the first steps towards a model which could bring together all education and training programmes within one framework, with potential benefits to both individuals and the economy.

The book draws heavily on developments promoted and supported by the Manpower Services Commission (now Training Agency) and the National Council for Vocational Qualifications. I am indebted to both these organisations in which I have worked during the mid- and late 1980s, respectively, and to numerous colleagues, researchers and consultants with whom I have worked. In producing the book, I am particularly indebted to Philippa Ingram who has done much to improve the readability of the text, to John Burke who has made many helpful suggestions and to Vini Jessup who proof-read the final text. I would also like to thank Alison Matthews, Nick Pnematicatos and Jean Eaborn who have helped to process successive drafts.

Finally, it must be emphasised that the interpretation of events and the views expressed in the book are mine and not necessarily those of the National Council.

Gilbert Jessup
October, 1990.

Part One
New Approaches, Methods and Instruments

1   Learning and Individuals

The measure of success for any education and training system should be what people actually learn from it, and how effectively. Just common sense you might think, yet this is a comparatively new idea.

Most writing and thinking about education and training is concerned with institutional arrangements, curriculum theory, the practice of teaching, staff development and so on.[1] A recent influential report from the CBI Task Force on Vocational Education and Training made a similar point:

> The debate on education and training in Britain has too often been concerned with structures and delivery and too little with contents and outcomes'.[2]

A German, writing on education in the UK, recently observed:

> Another peculiarity of the English tradition, is how little attention has been paid in pedagogical discussions to the contents of education. Most publications — above all most of the Royal Commission Reports on education — deal with school organization: whether or not, and for how long, education should be compulsory; and how the school system itself, once established should be organised and structured.[3]

We have what has been described as a provider-led system. What is frequently neglected is the learner, that is the client or customer of the education and training service.

If we start from the viewpoint of the individual on the receiving end, that is the student, the trainee or just the learner, we begin to recognise that learning is not confined to what education and training provides. Learning is a personal experience which can take many forms and can occur in many places. In fact we all learn all the time with varying degrees of efficiency. What we learn varies in its value to us as individuals and its general utility.

No one would dispute that we learn a great many things through experience in life rather than as part of our formal education and training. Nor would anyone question that what they acquire from an education or training programme is a personal and selective interpretation of the course which is offered.[4]

Nevertheless when one sits in conferences and seminars, or reads books on this subject, there seems to be an assumption that educators and trainers exert proprietary control over the process of learning.[5] Learning so is to be equated with what is provided in courses and programmes. One hears much about the need to provide a 'coherent learning experience', but the concept of coherence is usually limited to the particular package that the teacher is offering. Learning inputs always come in packages, whether these are subjects taught in schools, short management courses provided for employees or books or open learning programmes. Most packages assume that either the learner knows nothing before he or she starts, or that all have a common base of knowledge and skill.

Yet if anyone can exercise control over the process of learning, it is the individual, who might exercise a degree of control over their own learning. Similarly, coherence is ultimately a matter for the individual learner. It is only the learner who can make sense of the diverse inputs he or she receives and relate them to his or her perception of the world.

If learning is perceived from the viewpoint of the learner rather than that of the teacher or trainer, and more particularly those who manage the education and training industry, one has to change the conventional model and the concepts used. If one accepts that the central process with which we are concerned is learning, and that learning can take many forms, education and training may be seen as helping to make that possible. The focus on learning would also help to eradicate the distinction between education and training, and the establishments and agencies which divide learning into two camps. As a learner I do not make this distinction. My head does not have separate compartments to receive education and training.

The model developed in this book views education and training as the provision of learning opportunities. It is concerned about how we might create a national provision which is 'learner centred'. It does not presume that some modes of learning are superior to others, but suggests maximising the choice of opportunities. Individuals differ in the way they prefer to learn and in the time and opportunity they have available. In a customer oriented system, in which the learner is the customer, this should determine what is provided.

The model recognizes that learning can pursue general objectives of self-development, cultural development and intellectual development, or can pursue more specific objectives and be clearly instrumental in achieving defined goals. The former is more associated with education and the latter training. They are, of course, not mutually exclusive; much of education has instrumental value and training certainly contributes to self development. They are closely linked and at best enhance each other.[6] Either can be reduced to mindless rote learning (eg multiplication tables, history dates, sales procedures, machine maintenance checks) or benefit from a more reflective approach. The traditional distinction is unhelpful. No assumption is made here about the status of one form of learning compared with another.

Whether pursuing general or specific objectives individuals will learn more effectively if they are clear about the targets or outcomes they are trying to achieve. Learning is a purposeful activity and should be targeted on explicit outcomes.[6] This should not discourage unplanned, additional learning taking place en route, nor should it stop people following tangential lines of enquiry out of curiosity. In fact, such additional learning is more likely to be stimulated within the context of a learning plan.

The view, which often seems to prevail in education circles, that learning is simply 'good' for people and it does not matter much what they learn, is not accepted. Not only are some achievements much more important than others to an individual at any point in their lives, learning, like other forms of behaviour, is normally more efficient when goal directed, and when the learner is motivated to achieve the goal.

Current and past education and training practices have been pretty inefficient. Children squander an enormous amount of time in schools, often learning little and slowly. It is not even fun. As we all know, a significant minority of school leavers do not even acquire the basic skills for employment in relatively 'unskilled' work. The 'higher' objectives sought by teachers and others, such as the development of cultural and artistic interests, are not effectively realized for the majority of the young people.

Some aspects of education may even be counter-productive. For example, the way Shakespeare or poetry are taught in schools may actually put more people off these pursuits as adults than the number it stimulates to continue. This is not to question the aim of such education, only the outcome.

The majority of people are operating in employment, and in life generally, at far below their potential. This must be true if one compares what is being achieved in other countries, both in respect of the average educational levels reached by the population and their patterns of employment. There is no reason to believe that the distribution of intelligence or the inherent potential of the population in such countries is any higher than that of Britain. Nor is there any reason to think that the potential of the population has yet been maximised in these more advanced societies. Another comparison is to look back in our own society just a few generations ago. If I had been born a century or so earlier, I should probably have received little or no education and spent most of my life as an agricultural labourer, yet I would have had the same inherent potential for development as I had when born in the middle of the twentieth century.

We do not know the limits of human potential, or if there are any such limits, but we do know that most people in Britain are capable of a great deal more than is expected of them today.

The model presented in this book is learner centred and stems from a concern that individuals should be given the opportunity to realise their potential. Following directly from this is a second concern, that the country needs to make much more effective use of its human resource to remain economically competitive. The arguments for raising the levels of competence of the workforce, which have been rehearsed in many recent publications and speeches, are considered in the next chapter.

Happily, the needs of individuals to realise their potential, to develop their skills and knowledge, to take on more responsible and fulfilling work and to earn more money, seem to be largely compatible with the current needs of the country and the economy, for a workforce of more competent, responsible, flexible and autonomous employees. This is why the government, CBI, TUC and many other agencies, are all promoting very similar objectives on education and training. With the objectives largely agreed, the issue now is how to achieve them.

This book considers the form or structure of the education and training system to meet both the needs of individuals and those of the country. It looks at the framework which is required to make education and training more relevant and accessible to the whole population. It is not just concerned with young people but also adults, in employment and outside, many of whom never expect to participate in further education or training in their lives again. It is also concerned with the content of education and training needed to prepare people for a more dynamic industrial society in the twenty-first century.

Finally, there is growing recognition that a better educated society is more likely to be able to cope with environmental problems which threaten to overwhelm us in the next century.

2   National Needs and Problems

This chapter will not start by setting out the statistics on how we lag behind other industrial countries, and even emerging third world countries, in our participation rates in education and training and the levels we achieve. The picture has been effectively presented in numerous recent publications by the government,[1] the Labour Party,[2] the CBI,[3] the TUC[4] and many others.[5] Let us take this as given.

A flavour of the growing concern with the situation may be gained from some quotations from recent reports and speeches:

Education and training are at the top of nearly everyone's agenda for action. The skills of the United Kingdom workforce compare poorly with those of our principal competitors (CBI, 1989b).

There is a need for a quantum leap in the education and training of young people to meet both their aspirations and the needs of the economy in an increasingly competitive world (CBI, 1989a).

Britain is facing a skills challenge greater than any since the Industrial Revolution. Major changes in work, in the workforce, and in the global economy are creating the need to tap the potential of all our workers. By the year 2000, we will either be a superskills economy, or a low-skill, low pay society (TUC, 1989).

Education and training were now the 'commanding heights' of every modern economy ... Now and for all time in the future, human skills and human talents will be the major determinants of success or failure — not just for individuals but for a whole society in all its social, cultural and commercial life ... That was why investment in training would be the most important priority of all. (Neil Kinnock, October, 1989).

To summarize, in order to maintain its competitiveness in the international market place, British business must raise the skills profile of its workforce. Insofar as other countries are already ahead, Britain will need to improve its education and training performance even faster than its competitors (Training in Britain, 1989).

There are many who think we do not spend enough on education and training, which is no doubt true, but even within current levels of expenditure, we are not getting the most from what is spent. There are a variety of reasons for this. It is now widely recognized that our statutory education provision from age five to 16 years, fails to equip a significant minority of young people with the basic skills for employment, even in rudimentary jobs, for progression to vocational training and for a fulfilling life. Until recently the form of education for 14–16 year-olds, and the examination system at age 16, were designed for the minority who were to continue in full-time education through A levels and university. The system was actually designed to fail the majority of young people![6] This issue is now being addressed by the introduction of the National Curriculum which is considered in chapter 10.

The provision of education and training is fragmented, resulting in a difficult transition for young people from school to vocational education and training. Progression from vocational education and training to higher education is an even greater problem. Within vocational education and training itself, there exists no overall system, only numerous sub-systems which are constantly changing. The resulting discontinuities and overlaps are wasteful and inefficient, and also discourage people from continuing with education and training, often limiting their career prospects. The problem is confounded by the imposition of unnecessary entry restrictions to programmes and qualifications. These are some of the reasons for our low participation rates.

Numerous national initiatives, schemes and programmes to improve and extend vocational education and training in the UK have been implemented during the last few decades. Their impact has been felt in schools, further education and in industry. In recent years we can point to such programmes as the Youth Training Scheme (YTS), the Technical and Vocational Educational Initiative (TVEI), Employment Training (ET), the Certificate of Pre-vocational Education (CPVE), JTS, TOPs, REPLAN, PICKUP, Open Tec, the Open College and many more. But these initiatives do not relate to each other or add up to an overall national strategy or system of vocational education and training. Nor do these programmes effectively interface with GCSE, GCE 'A' levels, or previously, CSE and 'O' levels, or with higher education.

A proliferation of disparate schemes is not the most effective way of allocating national resources to education and training. Each new scheme tends to be devised from scratch with its own structure and content, delivery infrastructure, administrative machinery, funding criteria, forms, staff development, guidance materials, marketing, and so on. The unique features of each scheme are frequently emphasised, in a spirit of competition, rather than its similarity and relationship with other programmes. Employers, and even the educators and trainers running the schemes, have difficulty in understanding the ramifications of the different forms of provision, or the content and status of programmes and resulting certificates. Even more serious are the problems it creates for individuals, and their advisers, who wish to make best use of the opportunities on offer in planning their careers.

INSERT 1: EMPLOYERS AWARENESS OF TRAINING SCHEMES

Thames Valley TEC Chief Executive Gregory Hyland has carried out a poll amongst employers in the area. It found that 60 percent had heard of YTS and 60 percent had made use of it. As a check, Mr Hyland then invented a fictitious training scheme [the Manpower Training Scheme (MTS)]; 60 percent of employers said they had heard of it and 15 percent said they had used it.

'Most employers do not have a clue what is going on.' said Gregory Hyland. 'They are confused. There is a spaghetti soup of ideas out there. The job of the TEC is to make sure business knows what is on offer and what the issues are. You can only be successful in international competition if you have a high standard of training. We need people to get a bit more fire in their bellies.'

(reproduced from HRD News, July, 1990)

In conjunction with this complex mass of education and training provision, we have an equally complex and untidy array of vocational qualifications. A free market has operated in vocational qualifications and several independent national systems have grown up, some well established such as those of City and Guilds and the Royal Society of Arts, dating back over a hundred years. The Business and Technician Education Council, the other major body, is a more recent creation of the government. The London Chamber of Commerce Institute and Pitmans also have well established qualification systems operating primarily in the business and commercial fields. In addition, there are regional bodies and a wide range of industry bodies offering awards within their sectors, and of course there are hundreds of professional bodies. There is no agreement between them on the form, size, shape or status of qualifications, or the terms used to describe them or the processes involved in their award. It is not surprising that our system, or lack of system, has been frequently described as the 'qualification jungle'.

The shortcomings of the vocational qualification provision was summed up by the government's Review of Vocational Qualifications in 1986 and is shown in insert 2.

INSERT 2: THE SHORTCOMINGS OF EXISTING ARRANGEMENTS

(from the Review of Vocational Qualifications, MSC, 1986)

i)   there is no clear, readily understandable pattern of provision;

ii)   there are gaps in provision;

iii) there are considerable areas of actual or apparent overlap both within and between the three parts of the system [examining and validating bodies, professional bodies, industry bodies]. This overlap and duplication can be wasteful and inefficient;

iv)   arrangements for progression and transfer are often not well defined or practicable;

v)   there are many barriers to access arising from attendance and entry requirements for courses, membership regulations, or the inflexible pattern of examination schedules;

vi)   assessments carried out by many bodies do not adequately test or record the competences required in employment;

vii) assessment methods tend to be biased towards the testing either of knowledge or of skill rather than of competence;

viii) there is insufficient recognition of learning acquired in non-formal situations;

ix)   there is often insufficiently rapid response to ever changing needs, and

x)   for whatever reason (and the cause on occasion must be the perceived inadequacy or partial relevance of a qualification) there is a very limited take-up of vocational qualifications in some important occupational areas, for example, in the distribution industry.

The need for a fundamental re-orientation in vocational education and training to meet the needs of changing work patterns in a technological age was well recognized by some at the beginning of the last decade, and no doubt long before. The Manpower Services Commission's New Training Initiative in 1981[6] stated that if the UK was to meet its training needs in a rapidly changing and increasingly competitive economic environment, we needed a workforce which was both more highly skilled and more flexible. Employees would need to train and retrain throughout their working lives to keep pace with changing work requirements and occupational structures. New Training Initiative set out an alternative approach which underlies the new model of education and training which is now being introduced.

Some aspects of the New Training Initiative (NTI) were introduced in the early 1980s, such as the Youth Training Scheme and TVEI, to increase the vocational provision for young people. The NTI also spawned a number of adult training initiatives, but these were piecemeal and led to the problems outlined above. There was little general understanding of how to produce the new 'flexible and adaptable' worker, although there were many proposals and projects. NTI signalled the end of traditional apprenticeship training, which relied on time serving rather than the achievement of standards, but an alternative was not immediately available.

The most significant feature of the New Training Initiative was the introduction of a new concept of 'standards', although its significance was little understood by readers in 1981. The key sentence was tucked away in the middle of the report — 'at the heart of this initiative lie standards of a new kind'. Today those 'new kind of standards' lie at the heart of the new model of education and training which is the subject of this book.

Although the NTI contained the foundations on which to build, the new model was slow to develop as the form of the new standards was not clear, nor was there a methodology for deriving them. While the NTI provided an excellent basis by setting out the principles and objectives to be achieved, translating them into practice still remained a major problem.

The first faltering attempts to formulate standards, which can be directly linked to the NTI proposal, are recorded in 1983.[7] They represented such a radical departure from most existing practice that they were initially not well received. These first attempts at formulating standards are shown in chapter 5, which illustrates how the current methodology evolved.

The New Training Initiative, particularly those aspects which bear on standards, is worthy of re-examination. An MSC paper written in March, 1985, has been reproduced in full at Appendix A. The paper restates the objectives proposed in the New Training Initiative and begins to show how they could be put into effect within a system of standard setting, assessment and accreditation. The origin of many of the later recommendations made by the Review of Vocational Qualifications (MSC, 1986) and subsequently put into practice by the National Council for Vocational Qualifications, can be seen in that paper.

The major impact of the 'new kind of standards' which are being introduced is that they make explicit the outcomes sought in education and training programmes. This contrasts with most previous forms of education and training provision which has been defined in respect of learning 'inputs' in the form of syllabuses, courses, training specifications and so on. The requirements of qualifications have also been based primarily on the content of the syllabuses and training specifications, and not the other way around. This shift from an input-led system to an outcome-led system has fundamental implications, both in defining the content of education and training and in opening access to different modes of learning. The specification of outcomes provides the key to unlocking the education and training system.

By specifying learning objectives, in the form of outcome standards, independent of any course, programme or mode of learning, it becomes possible to create a framework of such standards, which can be adopted by any course or programme. The standards provide the unifying concept for all learning. A framework of standards provides the reference grid within which different forms of learning provision can be related.

In order that people can achieve the standards, and have their achievement recorded, the standards are 'packaged' in the form of units of credit and qualifications. Qualifications in the new system are defined as groups of units of credit — groupings which relate to occupational requirements. By labelling and classifying the units and qualifications the relationship between them can be perceived.

The transition to a standards-based or outcome-led system can be seen in the vocational education and training system through the introduction of National Vocational Qualifications (NVQs). It can also be seen in schools through the introduction of the National Curriculum.

The shift to an outcome-led system of education and training thus means a qualification-led or assessment-led system. This proposition makes a lot of people unhappy because they think of qualifications as 'sitting exams' and writing essays or doing multiple-choice tests. If this were to be the case I would share their concern. Educationalists are also unhappy with the proposition because they believe that qualifications do not and cannot assess many of the finer aspects of the learning that they believe to be important. They are right if they think only in terms of traditional forms of qualifications. But this is not what is now being proposed for the new standards-based qualifications.

Along with the new standards must go new forms of assessment, very different from sitting examinations. The full benefits of the model can only be realized if assessment can cover all the things we want people to learn (and more importantly what the learners want to learn). It also only works if assessment is more friendly and facilitates learning rather than acting as a deterrent or just an obstacle to be overcome.

We are therefore talking about new kinds of standards and new forms of assessment. This also implies new forms of learning (see insert 3). The other feature is how the standards, assessment and learning, and the other features we shall be describing, relate to each other. That is what is meant by a model. This book attempts to describe the characteristics of the new model.

INSERT 3: 'NEW' APPROACHES AND MODELS

Many readers of this book from within the education and training profession will no doubt be offended when I refer to reforms, new practices and new models. They will say 'we do that already, its not new!' and I will have to admit that is so. The outcome-led model outlined here, with all its ramifications, is of course built upon a lot of good practice in education and training. It attempts to bring together most of the progressive developments in education and training which have developed over recent decades, particularly during the 1980s, and weld them into a coherent national system.

Features such as unit credits and modular delivery are not new but they are still not normal practice. Individualized learning has no doubt been around as long as individuals, but few parts of the education and training system fully cope with the unique needs of individuals. I know that individual action planning is now being practised in many locations, but how well is it being done and can the institutions and organisations to which trainees subsequently go deliver what is expected?

So when practices are described in this book as new, please accept that they will certainly be new to a lot of people. If they are already part of your everyday life, take credit in that it is your experience upon which the 'new' model is being designed. Similarly, if changes are described as 'radical' or 'reforms' or even 'revolutionary', believe me that is the way they will appear to lots of people, even if you have already taken them in your stride.

Some of the practices advocated in this book cannot be achieved by individual tutors and trainers alone, or even the institutions and authorities they represent. They can only come about by changes at national level through changes in the collective policies and practices of awarding bodies, industry bodies, professional bodies and government.

What is new is the overall model. No one yet operates it in full since many of the bits are not yet in place to be used. Many institutions and programmes are beginning to institute parts of the model.

The term 'model' might sound pretentious. Purists would no doubt say it is not a model anyway. I use the term to emphasise that we are not simply considering a set of good practices, but that there is a coherent philosophy behind what is being proposed and an inherent logic about the way the bits fit together. Once you take the first step, making explicit the outcomes of learning required, the other bits fall into place.

It is interesting to observe that the 'revolutionaries' who are advocating these changes in education and training are not groups shouting in the streets but the CBI, the TUC, the government and the Labour Party. I use the word 'revolution' advisedly as this was the term in the recent, influential report from the CBI, 'Towards a skills revolution' (CBI, 1989). The recommendations in that report are totally consistent with the model described here.

INSERT 4: THE REVIEW OF VOCATIONAL QUALIFICATIONS

A significant step towards the new model was made by the Review of Vocational Qualifications. The review was carried out by a working group set up by the government in April, 1985 (DE/DES 1985) which reported a year later (MSC/DES 1986). It recommended the development of standards, picking up the concept from the New Training Initiative, new forms of qualifications, to be described as National Vocational Qualifications (NVQs), and the creation of a new framework for such qualifications, the NVQ framework. It also recommended the setting up of a new body to carry through these proposals, the National Council for Vocational Qualifications (NCVQ). These proposals were rapidly endorsed by government in the 1986 White Paper 'Education and Training — Working Together'.

National Vocational Qualifications

NCVQ was formally established in October 1986 as an independent body, initially funded by the government, to implement the remit set out in the White Paper. The remit covered England, Wales and Northern Ireland, but not Scotland, which has an independent education system. NCVQ has no legal powers and can only effect change with the co-operation of awarding bodies, industry bodies, professional bodies and numerous other agencies which are part of the standards/qualifications/education/training infrastructure. NCVQ relies on 'marketing' the concept of NVQs and gaining general support for the reform process. It also relies on the government to use its influence to support the introduction of NVQs. The funding and management of the programme to stimulate industry to set standards for NVQs was retained by the government, operating first through the MSC, then the Training Agency.

NCVQ have set criteria which qualifications are required to meet in order to be incorporated in the new national framework. The criteria provide the design specification for National Vocational Qualifications and the mechanism for controlling what is accepted in the framework. The NVQ criteria are reviewed in detail in the next chapter as they make many aspects of the proposed model explicit. The 'new kinds of standards' advocated in the New Training Initiative are now being put into effect through the introduction of NVQs.

We shall also see in chapter 10 how similar approaches to specifying the outcomes of learning have been adopted in the National Curriculum.

3   National Vocational Qualifications

Vocational education and training is being radically reorganised through the introduction of National Vocational Qualifications (NVQs). NVQs will be offered through existing examining and validating bodies, professional bodies and industry training organizations, but all NVQs must conform to a common set of criteria. It is through the mechanism of applying common criteria in accrediting NVQs that qualifications are being aligned within one national framework. The criteria are thus worthy of close examination.

Definition

An NVQ is defined as:

> a statement of competence clearly relevant to work and intended to facilitate entry into, or progression in, employment and further learning, issued to an individual by a recognized awarding body.

> The statement of competence should incorporate specified standards in:

> — the ability to perform in a range of work related activities

> and

> — the underpinning skills, knowledge and understanding required for performance in employment.

(All quotations in this chapter are taken from NVQ Criteria and Procedures, NCVQ, 1989).

The NVQ statement of competence provides a target for people and programmes to aim at. The NVQ certificate is a statement of competence of what an individual has achieved.

The two aspects of the statement of competence which the definition goes on to add are significant, as is their relationship to each other. The statement leads on 'performance', which is of course central to the concept of competence, and places 'skills, knowledge and understanding' as underpinning requirements of such performance. This does not deny the need for knowledge and understanding, but does make clear that they, however necessary, are not the same thing as competence. This has considerable implications for assessment.

The Statement of Competence

A statement of competence must meet certain technical requirements if it is to fulfil the functions for which it is designed. It must also be presented in a common format if it is to be easily recognised and relate to other statements within a national system. For these reasons the NVQ criteria state:

> The NVQ statement of competence must be set out in a format which has the three following levels of detail:
>
> — NVQ title;
> — units of competence;
> — elements of competence, with their associated performance criteria

The criteria go on to say:

> The NVQ title should denote the area of competence encompassed by the qualification and its level. It provides the means by which the qualification is located in the NVQ framework.
>
> A unit of competence consists of a coherent group of elements of competence and associated performance criteria which form a discrete activity or sub-area of competence which has meaning and independent value in the area of employment to which the NVQ relates.

The format of the statement of competence is shown in insert 5 and illustrated by examples in chapter 5.

The performance criteria provide the standards by which performance, as described by the elements of competence, are assessed. Elements of competence, which provide the detailed specifications of competence in the system, plus their performance criteria, are thus the basic bricks from which statements of competence are built.

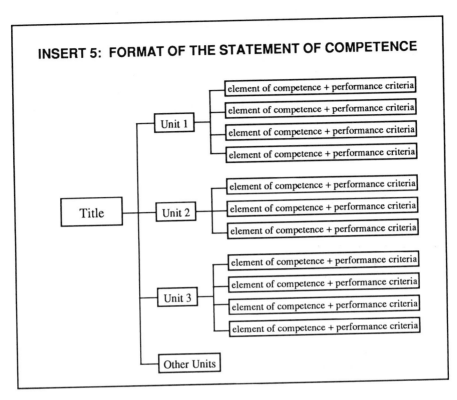

INSERT 5: FORMAT OF THE STATEMENT OF COMPETENCE

The NVQ criteria state:

The elements and performance criteria should:

— be stated with sufficient precision to allow unambiguous interpretation by different users, eg awarding bodies, assessors, trainers, and candidates;
— not be so detailed that they only relate to a specific task or job, employer or organisation, location or equipment.

This last statement touches on the issue of the 'breadth' of competence, a matter of considerable debate, which is considered in chapter 4.

The statement of competence spells out what candidates are required to demonstrate for the award of an NVQ, and includes the performance criteria against which performance is judged. In doing so, the statements of competence also set clear goals for education and training programmes. The specification of competence plus performance criteria provide the operational realisation of the 'new kind of standards'.

Employment-led

The NVQ statements of competence are derived, not from an analysis of education and training programmes or the preconceptions of educators and trainers, but from a fresh analysis of present day employment requirements. Moreover, it is the employers and employees in the relevant industrial sector, occupation or profession, who have responsibility for saying what the requirements for qualifications, and thus training, are. The NVQ criteria state:

> The statement of competence for an NVQ should be determined and/or endorsed by an acceptable group with responsibility for maintaining and improving national standards of performance in the sectors(s) of employment where the competence is practised.

The 'acceptable groups' who are setting the standards are described as 'industry lead bodies'. There are some 150 such bodies now setting the standards within their sectors (see chapter 6).

Assessment

Assessment in NVQs is based directly on the statement of competence. Assessment poses the question of whether the statement of competence has been achieved or not. As candidates do not have to undergo any particular programme of learning, the award of an NVQ is based solely on the outcome of assessment. As assessment is such a significant issue in NVQs the criteria and implications are considered separately in chapter 7. The requirements are summarised in the primary criterion:

> Assessment may be regarded as the process of collecting evidence and making judgements on whether performance criteria have been met. For the award of an NVQ a candidate must have demonstrated that he or she can meet the performance criteria for each element of competence specified.

Considerable emphasis is placed on the assessment of performance in NVQs, as competence is about being able to perform. This has resulted in a growth of assessment in the workplace, where occupational competence is most often demonstrated. This has major implications for the form and location of vocational education and training in the future.

The direct involvement of employers and employees in determining the statements of competence is to ensure that training is relevant to future employment requirements. The other key concept in the design of NVQs is concerned with access.

Access

The NVQ criteria state:

NVQ awards should be free from any barriers which restrict access
to them and should be independent of:

— the mode of learning. This is made possible by the form of an
NVQ, which is independent of any education or training programme which may be provided to develop competence;
— upper and lower age limits, except where legal restraints make
this necessary. Assessment for the award of NVQs should be
open to people of all ages;
— a specified period of time to be spent in education, training or
work before the award can be made. NVQs should not prescribe
the time taken to acquire competence. This recognises the considerable variation in the time individuals take to learn, depending
on their starting point, learning opportunities, aptitude and
motivation.

Open access is made easier through making NVQs independent of any
form of learning provision. It is perhaps hardly necessary to say that there
should be no unnecessary restrictions on candidates being assessed for an
award, except that such restrictions have often been placed on qualifications
in the past. Entry to many occupations, for example, has been severely
restricted by apprenticeship schemes in which entry is limited to a particular
age, and qualification is only achieved after a specified period of time.[1]
Insert 6 illustrates how both assessment and learning are based on the
statement of competence, but are conceptually independent of each other.
This has important implications for opening access.
NCVQ goes further and positively encourages the following:

— the availability of different modes of learning to increase the opportunities people have in participating in education and training. It also
encourages flexibility in provision so that fast learners can make rapid
progress while those who need longer have the extra time and tuition
available. This factor, combined with the recognition that the needs
of individuals will differ depending upon prior experience and future
aspirations, points to individualised learning programmes;
— the availability of different modes of assessment, where this is technically feasible and practicable. For example, if workplace assessment
is the predominant mode for an NVQ, people without access to an
appropriate workplace will be debarred unless assessment is also
available off the job. This may involve simulating the primary work

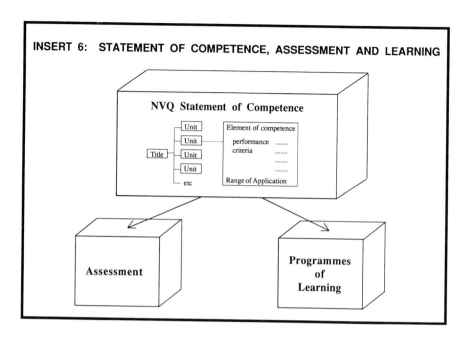

INSERT 6: STATEMENT OF COMPETENCE, ASSESSMENT AND LEARNING

NVQ Statement of Competence

Title — Unit, Unit, Unit, Unit, etc

Element of competence

performance ....
criteria ....
....
....

Range of Application

Assessment

Programmes of Learning

requirements in a college or training workshops in order that candidates can practice and demonstrate their competence, or setting up competency tests, or both. These alternatives are discussed in chapter 7;

— particular consideration for candidates with special needs, such as physical or sensory disabilities. If they can demonstrate they could cope with the employment requirements represented by units or NVQs, by whatever means, they should be eligible to gain the appropriate award. This may mean allowing special aids or creating special arrangements for assessment. The NVQ unit-credit arrangements are helpful in allowing access to one or more unit credits for those who might not be able to gain a full NVQ.[2]

Unit-Credits and Credit Accumulation

One reason why the NVQ statement of competence requires units of competence to be created is to satisfy another criterion:

Units should be designed so that they may be offered for separate assessment and recording as credits within the national credit accumulation and transfer system.

The formal certification of unit-credits is another significant feature of NVQs. This provides a framework for learning and accreditation of smaller 'chunks' of competence. It also allows considerable flexibility in the design of programmes of learning or individual action plans. Credits can be accumulated from assessment in different locations and through different modes. These features further enhance access to qualifications. Unit credits and the national credit accumulation and transfer system based upon them are considered in detail in chapter 9.

The NVQ Framework

The framework is being created by allocating NVQs as they become accredited by NCVQ to an area of competence and a level within a unified national system. The framework has until recently been limited to four levels, spanning qualifications from the most basic to those approximating to higher national within existing systems. In March 1990, following extensive consultations with professional bodies and other interest groups, the framework was extended to include level 5. During the 1990s we can thus expect the gradual incorporation of professional qualifications within the NVQ framework. The government has expressed the intention that the NVQ framework should be comprehensive and include vocational and professional qualifications at all levels and in all areas. Priority is being given to establishing NVQs at levels 1 to 4, and the target date for achieving this is December 1992.

There is no precise way of allocating NVQs to levels within the framework. As the competence requirements become more 'demanding' at higher levels within an occupation, the nature of the competence changes in a number of ways.[3] These are expressed in the NVQ criteria publication as follows:

The higher the level of a qualification the more of the following characteristics it is likely to have:

— breadth and range of competence;
— complexity and difficulty of competence;
— requirement for special skills;
— ability to undertake specialized activity;
— ability to transfer competences from one context or work environment to another;
— ability to innovate and cope with non–routine activities;
— ability to plan and organize work;
— ability to supervise others.

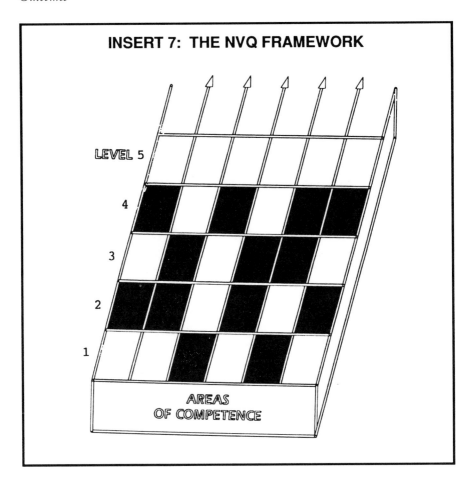

INSERT 7: THE NVQ FRAMEWORK

LEVEL 5

4

3

2

1

AREAS
OF COMPETENCE

It might also have added that the body of knowledge on which competent performance depends is likely to increase. This is thought to be a particular feature of level 5 qualifications, most of which are currently underpinned by higher education degrees.

The level definitions offered by NCVQ are shown in insert 8.

The primary purpose of the NVQ framework is to facilitate transfer and progression, both within occupational areas and between them. This is being achieved by grouping together those qualifications that are similar in their statements of competence. Through a process of rationalisation, functions which appear in different occupations or industrial sectors (eg information processing, cash handling, customer services, reception duties) should be expressed in units which are common to those different occupations or industries. Thus qualifications will often share common units providing indications of routes of progression and transfer between different areas.

INSERT 8: NVQ LEVELS

The following definitions provide a guide to the levels at which NVQs may be accredited within the framework. They are intended to be indicative rather than prescriptive: —

— Level I: competence in the performance of work activities which are in the main routine and predictable or provide a broad foundation, primarily as a basis for progression;

— Level II: competence in a broader and more demanding range of work activities involving greater individual responsibility and autonomy than at Level I;

— Level III: competence in skilled areas that involve performance of a broad range of work activities, including many that are complex and non-routine. In some areas, supervisory competence may be a requirement at this level;

— Level IV: competence in the performance of complex, technical, specialised and professional work activities, including those involving design, planning and problem solving, with a significant degree of personal accountability. In many areas competence in supervision and management will be a requirement at this level;

— Level V: competence in all professional areas above that of level IV (yet to be formally defined).

Although the NVQ framework is commonly presented in two dimensions, it finds a more sophisticated representation in the NCVQ computer database which contains details of all NVQs, including the statements of competence. In the database, NVQs and units are also classified by occupation and industry, which allows progression routes to be explored by individuals and their advisers in a variety of ways. The NVQ database provides an important new tool in the implementation of the new model of education and training.

The framework classification system of NVQs according to areas of competence is still being developed but the form it will take and the primary categories have been agreed. A current draft is shown at Appendix 'C'.

To summarize, the primary features of NVQs are formalized through the criteria set for NVQs, which require a statement of competence in a given format and assessment in relation to that statement. Employment relevance is achieved by ensuring the statement of competence is determined and/or endorsed by industry. Access to NVQs is maximised by the absence of restrictions on eligibility to assessment, and in particular the independence of assessment from programmes of learning. Unit credits also enhance access and provide flexibility in learning provision. The NVQ framework is designed to provide progression and transfer between qualifications, within and between occupational areas, and coherence in the education and training provision.

4   The Concept of Competence

If statements of competence are to determine the standards for qualifications and, as a result the form and content of the future provision of vocational education and training, it is of considerable significance how we view competence. There has been a continuing debate on this issue as the programme has expanded.[1] As described earlier, a shift has taken place from the determination of competence primarily by those in the educational sector (further education and awarding bodies) to those in the industrial sector (employers and employees), through the network of industry bodies. Many educationalists fear that this will result in a narrow concept of competence, based upon the immediate job requirements. In truth, this trend has been apparent in some industries, where the statements of competence set reflect the current, often narrow jobs which people perform. Considerable effort is now being exerted by NCVQ, the Training Agency, the CBI and others advising industry lead bodies, to broaden this concept of competence.

Before we look at what is meant by 'breadth', we should perhaps clarify that the term 'competent', as used here, does not refer to a lowish or minimum level of performance. On the contrary, it refers to the standard required successfully to perform an activity or function. In manufacturing this would relate to quality control standards required to produce a satisfactory product. In the performance of a service, it means meeting the requirements of a customer or client. In most employment areas, unlike education, there is a recognized standard of performance related to the concept of 'quality'. Being competent means performing to professional or occupational standards. In most professional and occupational areas there is no scope for 'second best' standards.

The Requirement for 'Breadth'

The origins of the current NVQ programme lie in the New Training Initiative (MSC, 1981), in which the concept of 'new kinds of standards' was closely related to the need for a flexible and adaptable workforce. The thrust of NTI was the need to prepare people for careers which would be characterised by changing technology and job structures, and for much greater occupational mobility than employees had experienced in the past. This aspect of education and training has been emphasised more recently in the CBI publication '*Towards a Skills Revolution*'. The CBI are seeking a broad foundation of competence in all young people, though not only young people, upon which individuals can build throughout their life.[2]

While those who take a national perspective stress the need for breadth in both general education and training, many employers train for more specific and immediate needs. This potential conflict of interest becomes a particular problem if employers are expected both to specify the standards required for vocational education and training, and to play a major role in providing the related training. Many employers do of course take a longer term view of human resource development and encourage their employees to broaden their competence beyond the immediate requirements of their current jobs, but this is not yet a generally accepted practice.

National and Occupational Standards

Those employers and employees representing their occupational sector in industry lead bodies are being encouraged to take a national perspective and set broad based standards. Breadth is implicit in the concept of 'national' standards. A national standard for an employment function implies that it is generally applicable to all companies and contexts where that function is performed. It would thus normally be more general and broader than the expression of a standard which applied only to a particular company. The concept of occupational or professional competence has similar connotations. A person who is described as competent in an occupation or profession is considered to have a repertoire of skills, knowledge and understanding which he or she can apply in a range of contexts and organisations. To say that a person is competent in a 'job', on the other hand, may mean that their competence is limited to a particular role in a particular company.

The distinction between job competence or occupational/professional competence will depend on how broad or narrow the job is, and the variation in practice that occurs in different jobs in the same occupational category. The next chapter shows how the variation between jobs is taken into account in writing statements of competence.

Competence in a Role

Training for occupations or professions has tended to concentrate upon the technical requirements of jobs, the skills and tasks that need to be performed, while often neglecting the wider aspects of performance required to fulfil a work role. Thus engineers may be competent at solving engineering problems but poor at communicating their solutions to others. Secretaries may be efficient at typing, shorthand, filing, but not good at judging the priorities between these activities in meeting the broader objectives of their work role. Doctors may be able to diagnose the condition of patients, and know what treatments to prescribe, but lack skills in dealing with patients, or colleagues and staff.

Anyone who has worked knows that there is far more to being successful in a job than carrying out the basic tasks competently. Jobs are seldom performed in isolation. One has to work with other people, often solving problems or completing tasks as members of a team. One has to relate to people at a variety of levels on social and organizational matters, in addition to the performance of the functions specific to one's occupation. One also has to manage one's own job and cope with unexpected events which fall outside the practices and procedures of routine activities. To survive and flourish in organizations, particularly at senior levels, one needs to be politically sensitive and astute. It is often these less tangible aspects of competence rather than their technical skills, that distinguish between the successful and less successful employees.

The emphasis on this broader concept of role competence leads to increased demands for demonstrations of competence in the workplace in order to collect valid evidence for assessment. It also points to the need for work experience to be a component of most training which leads to occupational competence. In addition, the experience of work will need to be structured and varied to ensure sufficient coverage of the major components of competence described above. The alternative is far more extensive and imaginative practical work, project work or other forms of simulation, in colleges and training centres.

These aspects of competence which go beyond the technical have been been classified, under the headings 'task management', 'contingency management' and 'role/environment skills'. This has been described as the 'job competence model.'[3] All are considered necessary to be fully competent in an occupation or profession. How these are built into statements of competence still presents something of a challenge, but there are some good examples now emerging, as the next chapter illustrates.

Functional Analysis

The analysis and specification of competence according to functions, which is now advocated, provides a broader conception of competence than earlier task analysis approaches. The concentration on function shifts the focus of competence from tasks and procedures to the purpose and outcome of work activity. These are more likely to endure as technology and work procedures change. There is also less likelihood of neglecting the non–technical aspects of competence, insofar as these are required to achieve a successful outcome.

Knowledge

The 'breadth' of competence is intimately tied up with the question of knowledge and understanding, which has been central to the debate surrounding NVQs in educational circles. The new emphasis placed on competence and performance is often believed to be at the expense of knowledge and understanding. These issues are considered more fully in relation to assessment in later chapters, but an understanding of the principles underlying competent performance (ie why one does it that way) and a knowledge of how performance will need to vary to meet different circumstances, would seem to be minimum requirements of NVQs at any level. It is recognized that these simple requirements result in a large body of knowledge at professional levels.

The requirements for knowledge and understanding which underpin competence in NVQs should be derived afresh from the statement of competence. This provides a clear rationale for what needs to be acquired, which has often been lacking in previous systems. It is not clear whether this will result in more or less demands for knowledge, but whatever is required will be directly relevant to performance in an occupational or professional area. (For further discussion of knowledge and its assessment, see chapters 7 and 18).

Knowledge is an assessment issue in NVQs and the requirements are not spelled out directly in the statement of competence (see chapters 7 and 18).

Preparation for Change

Closely related to the issue of developing broadly competent people for current roles, is the need to prepare people for change in the future. How can we not only train people for the jobs they have to do now, but also give them a basis of competence to cope with, or acquire quickly, the skills they will need for work they might be performing in two years or five years from now? The approaches adopted to broaden the statement of competence described above are also relevant here. Specifying competence in respect to employment functions and outcomes, is helpful for they are less likely to change than the technology, the methods and procedures for achieving those outcomes.

The emphasis placed upon task management, contingency management and role/environment skills, encourages the development of the 'process' or core skills associated with employment, which are likely to endure and remain relevant as technology and work practices change.

As we have noted assessment in NVQs includes the requirement that candidates know how to apply their skills over the range of contexts. One aspect of this will normally be the assessment of their grasp of the underlying principles which govern the required behaviour. NVQs are thus likely to demand a body of knowledge and understanding which would form a basis for the acquisition of new skills.

A final point on preparing people for the future is that lead bodies setting standards should consider incorporating the more advanced technological practices in the occupational field in their specifications for NVQs, even though these may not yet have been introduced to many people's jobs.

Progression

A further consideration in preparing people for the future, is the extent to which one NVQ can provide a base for progression to another, at the next level in the same and related occupational areas. While doing this, we must be careful not to add extra requirements to an NVQ which might debar people who do not intend to take the next step from gaining a qualification at the level at which they are otherwise competent. The need is to develop competence at the appropriate occupational level in such a way that it both enhances practice at that level and also serves as a basis for progression.

The most effective way to achieve this is to pursue the approaches outlined above. A functional specification of competence, the assessment of knowledge and the underpinning principles, the inclusion of the broader role competences and the identification and enhancement of core skills are all likely to facilitate progression.

Core Skills

The problem of breadth is not limited to vocational training. Many consider our general education system, especially post-16, is too specialized and narrow as a preparation for employment and adult life. This was illustrated recently by the education minister, John MacGregor, in his request to the National Curriculum Council and Schools Examinations and Assessment Council to incorporate core skills in A/AS levels:

> There is a second issue, which covers a number of points raised by the Council about the 'vocational' dimension. I believe that whether they go into employment direct or via higher education, all students need to be equipped to take their place in a modern economy, as well as to be competent in every way to function in adult life generally. Specialism at A level, and the maintenance of rigorous standards, is

vitally important. But it must not, and need not, be at the expense of developing the broader skills, knowledge and understanding which will be needed in the twenty-first century. (MacGregor, 1989).

The issue of broadening A/AS levels, and NVQs, through the incorporation of core skills is considered in chapter 11. An approach to broaden both general education and training now underway is to identify and enhance the 'core' skills which underpin competent performance. By core skills, people normally refer to problem solving, communication, numeracy, personal effectiveness, and so on, those components of competence which are common to most activity, in employment or outside. (These components have also been referred to as generic competences, general competences, process skills and common learning outcomes in the recent debate).

Training in core skills is by no means a new idea, but the methods now adopted for stating competence and attainment offer new possibilities in formulating core skill requirements and giving credit for their attainment. This offers the potential for both enhancing education and training and, as core skills are fundamental to both, linking education and training systems. The essential feature of core skills is their potential transferability from one context to another seemingly very different one. The role of core skills in education and training is discussed in some detail in chapter 11.

It is sufficient, here, to recognize that identifying and assessing the core skills inherent in occupational competence provide another means of broadening NVQs and vocational training and making employees more flexible and adaptable.[4]

In summary, the concept of competence upon which NVQs are based is fundamental to future vocational and professional training. As it derives from the needs of employment, both present and future, the debate really centres upon how we perceive those needs. There are those who argue we must take a strategic view, and use the training and qualification system to shape the future. But others are, understandably, concerned with more immediate needs and do not yet share the long term view.

5 Statements of Competence and Standards

In a model of education and training in which both the learning provision and assessment are governed by the statement of competence, the way in which that statement is formulated is of crucial importance. We have seen in the last chapter the various aspects of competence that we wish to build into the statement. In this chapter we look at the state of the art in putting this into operation.

Background

The current methodology can be better understood if we look briefly at its evolution. The origins of the current work on standards development or specifying competence can be traced directly back to the New Training Initiative (1981) which set out the objectives for the new kinds of standards. The first attempt to put into operation these standards took the form of 'standard tasks', which were first designed to provide targets and assessment for workplace learning in the Youth Training Scheme.[1] The need for a precise description of a task or activity and the criteria for success became clear.

It was recognized as early as 1984 that standard tasks should be grouped into 'modules of accreditation'. The Action Plan in Scotland, adopted a modular system for Non-Advanced Further Education also in 1984, and the flexibility which such a system could provide was recognised. The first attempt to create a formal work based qualification system based on this methodology was in 1985, when MSC contracted with the Hotel and Catering Training Board, to develop what subsequently became CATERBASE.[3] Similar initiatives were started in clothing manufacture and meat processing, in the same year.

Standard tasks gave way to 'competence objectives' in 1986 and subsequently, when the NVQ criteria were first published, the current term 'element of competence' was adopted. Parallel developments in the 1980s

INSERT 9: THE DEFINITION OF STANDARD TASKS
(MSC, 1984)[2]

Standard Tasks are defined in occupational terms and in a standardized form. They contain:

— a title;

— a precise description of the task, including, as appropriate, objectives, conditions, equipment available etc.;

— a precise statement of the criteria for the successful performance of the task. These are presented as far as possible in the form of outputs which can be easily recognized by the trainees supervisor/tutor. All criteria must be met if the trainee is to be credited in that task.

had pursued similar routes, mainly to spell out the objectives of particular programmes. These were variously termed 'learning objectives', 'learning outcomes', 'profile statements' and so on. However, these approaches seldom adopted performance criteria and assessment consequently lacked rigour or fell back on traditional methods. The experiments in educational assessment in 'criterion-referencing' and the development of 'grade related criteria' represent further attempts to state the outcomes of learning.

Elements of Competence

NVQ statements of competence have adopted the term 'element of competence' (often called simply element) for the basic statements. Elements of competence are the most detailed descriptions within the new competence based system and those to which standards are attached. Elements of competence should have the following structure:

ACTIVE VERB   OBJECT   CONDITIONS

an example from catering might be:

maintain   standards of hygiene   in food preparation areas

or from medicine:

assess   the physical condition of   by inspection
              the patient

Occasionally the third component is unnecessary if there are no conditions which apply.

Performance Criteria

Elements of competence always have associated performance criteria, which set out what must be achieved for the successful performance of the element. The performance criteria thus set the standard for competent performance. An example of an element with its associated performance criteria taken from accountancy is shown in insert 10.

INSERT 10: ELEMENT FROM THE UNIT: STORE MANAGEMENT/STOCK CONTROL

ELEMENT OF COMPETENCE: Establish and develop systems of stores accounting and control.

PERFORMANCE CRITERIA: Detailed procedures relating to the valuation of stock, work in progress and finished stock which conform to the organization's stated accounting policies are agreed with the appropriate staff and implemented.

Procedures for pricing materials, issues which reflect the nature of material flows throughout the operating system are established.

Effective systems of stores accounting and control are established, maintained and updated.

Performance criteria, like elements, also have their semantic structure. They should always contain a critical outcome and an evaluative statement. A critical outcome is something that has to be done for the function described by the element to be successfully achieved. An evaluative statement can be quantitative or qualitative (implemented, established, updated — see above example). Performance criteria should refer to successful outcomes of performance and not the procedures for carrying out the activity. Procedures can vary with circumstances, context or organization. We want learners to recognise that the purpose of an activity is to achieve a successful result and that procedures, methods, techniques are a means to that end and not an end in themselves. When unexpected circumstances occur the procedures are often not appropriate or not sufficient and the performer must improvise to achieve success. Coping with the unexpected is a crucial part of the concept of competence we are trying to foster.

Range Statements

A more recent extension to the methodology of stating competence is the introduction of range statements. Experience has shown that an element of competence is often open to different interpretations unless a more detailed specification is provided of what the element covers. Range statements simply indicate the range of application of an element. They are particularly useful in providing guidance of what needs to be covered in programmes of learning and what needs to be assessed.

Without range statements, there is a danger that the demonstration of an element in one context is regarded as sufficient evidence to attest to competence. Range statements remind users that NVQs are based on occupational competence and national standards. Attesting to competence in an NVQ implies that the candidate can perform in a range of organizations and contexts. The judgement as to whether evidence of competence in one situation, say the candidate's workplace, is sufficient to infer that he or she can perform the same function elsewhere, must be made with some model of skill transfer in mind.

In the case of driving, the assumption is made that if someone demonstrates they can drive one car competently, they can drive all cars (although not heavy goods vehicles). This is implied by the driving test for which a demonstration on one car is sufficient to gain a licence of competence to drive. The assumption is made that the variation in the skills required to drive different cars is relatively small, such that the skills acquired in driving one car will transfer to another with little difficulty.

The inference of transfer from the original context of assessment to other situations may sometimes be quite legitimate, if the circumstances change little from one situation to another. On the other hand practice in respect of other elements of competence may vary considerably, in which case further assessment would be required in different contexts. Alternatively, or additionally, a knowledge of the variation one can expect, and an understanding of the principles on which competent performance is based, may be sufficient to ensure skill transfer.

Range statements indicate to assessors (and of course trainers and trainees), the range of application to which the element is expected to apply, and provide the basis to judge what demonstrations of competence, knowledge and understanding are required to attest to competence.

An example of an element incorporating a range statement is shown in insert 11.

Range statements not only broaden what people might otherwise interpret as the requirement of an element, they can also be used to limit the range of application. The range statement sets boundaries which can be broad or narrow. It may be judged that the range of application of an element is too large if every contingency is allowed. In these circumstances it might be

---

INSERT 11: ELEMENT OF COMPETENCE FROM ESTATE AGENCY

Unit: Promote the sale of property available through the agency

Element:

Agree property requirements with applicant

Performance Criteria:

- applicants are acknowledged promptly and politely and treated in a manner which promotes goodwill
- applicants are encouraged to ask questions and seek clarification
- options and alternatives are offered to establish applicant's property requirements and reliability
- likely availability of property meeting the applicant's requirements is described honestly
- details agreed with applicant relating to type, price and preferred location of property are complete and recorded accurately and legibly
- complete details relating to applicant's preferred method of communicating about newly available property is recorded accurately and legibly
- complete details relating to applicant's current property position, timescale expectations and financial status are recorded accurately and legibly
- accurate and complete details (applicant requirements, method of communicating, completion timescale and financial status) are provided promptly to relevant staff in the agency

Range of Applications to which the element applies

- Range of applicant expectations *to include maintenance (ease or do it yourself), services available (nearby or remote), additional/alternative uses to present use, originality of features, quality of structure/fixtures/fittings*
- Range of potential applicant situations *to include first time buyer, buyer part of a chain, buyer with property to sell but not yet on market, cash sale, job move*
- Range of financial status *to include mortgage needed, mortgage already organised, cash sale, bridging loan required*
- Range of financial situations *to include low, medium and high earners; retired buyers; joint (equal) incomes*
- Range of market conditions *to include both "buyers market" and "sellers market"*

---

possible to divide the coverage between two elements with different range statements, possibly related to different levels within the NVQ framework.

Specifying range statements may in some cases be straightforward. It may be quite obvious, for instance, that in maintaining chemical plants there are three different types of pump with different characteristics, or that in preparing vegetables for cookery, there are a number of commonly encountered, but rather different, vegetables.

In other instances it may be helpful to ask WHAT IF questions to assist in identifying the required range. 'What if the employee transferred to a different site?'; 'What if the customer offered payment other than by cash?'; 'What if the menu changed?' 'What if we were to change suppliers?'

35

Looking at the various occupational areas, we can anticipate that the range of an element may apply to such dimensions as

- companies or organizations
- equipment
- materials
- work conditions and pressures
- customers or clients
- products
- services

This list provides only the common dimensions of range. Specialized occupational areas will include many other sources of variation.

Units of Competence

Units of competence consist of one or more elements, normally two, three or four. Units have a particular significance within the NVQ system because they are independently recognised and certificated. They are like 'mini qualifications'. A unit should be made up of a coherent group of elements which together are required to perform an employment function.

It is a matter of judgement as to the size of employment function which is chosen as a unit. It should be large enough to be worthy of separate recognition for a formal credit, that is a competence which would be valued by employers in the context of the occupation in which it is practised. On the other hand it should not be too large, or include elements of competence which trainees or employees might usefully acquire without needing the full requirement of the unit. Units also provide useful targets to aim at during the course of building up the competence required for a full NVQ. The accumulation of unit credits provides effective motivation for those undergoing programmes of learning, particularly for trainees who have not had much success in the past in formal examinations. The size of units will depend on the way in which work is organized within an occupational area. The size tends to increase with level in the NVQ framework, as employment at higher levels normally involves responsibility for larger and more complex functions.

An example of a unit of competence, with its constituent elements, performance criteria and range, is shown in insert 12.

Functional Analysis or Competence

The statements of competence are now being derived from an analysis of employment functions. The methodology, which is still being developed,

INSERT 12: UNIT OF COMPETENCE FROM HEALTH CARE SUPPORT

Unit:

Assist the client to achieve emotional comfort and rest

Element: Assist in minimising client discomfort and pain

Performance Criteria:
- the client is encouraged to express feelings of discomfort or pain, and is encouraged to use self-help methods to control these in accordance with the plan of care
- information agreed with the care team about pain or discomfort and ways in which it can be minimised, is given in a manner, and at a level and pace, appropriate to the client
- the client is assisted to maintain a comfortable position consistent with the plan of care and as agreed with the care team
- the client's condition is monitored in accordance with the plan of care
- requests from the client to minimise pain, or changes in the client's condition, are reported immediately to the appropriate member(s) of the care team and recorded accurately, legibly and completely in the appropriate document
- other clients disturbed by the client's pain and discomfort are given reassurance, as and when necessary

Range: Client groups: all
Care settings: all
All types of pain and discomfort

Element: Assist in providing conditions to meet the client's need for rest

Performance Criteria:
- the client is assisted to prepare and place him/herself in a position which is comfortable, is conducive to rest and is consistent with the plan of care
- as agreed with the care team and in accordance with organisational policy and practice, the client is assisted to take any prescribe medication as part of preparation for rest consistent with the plan of care
- the client is comforted, offered reassurance and encouraged to rest, through verbal and/or non-verbal means
- the client is monitored according to the plan of care and unusual circumstances are reported and/or recorded accurately
- the job-holder's own movements and behaviour are modified to assist the client's rest
- others entering the environment are reminded of the need to modify their behaviour and/or movements, if necessary
- adjustments are made to heating, ventilation, noise and light of environment to facilitate sleep rest as far as is possible
- environmental defects which interfere with client's rest are reported accurately and completely to the appropriate person and recorded, as and when required

Range: Client groups: all
Care settings: all

Element: contribute to the prevention and management of client distress

Performance criteria:
- where possible, client's belongings are placed according to his/her preferences
- behaviour which has previously indicated distress, or changes in the client's condition, are brought to the attention of the appropriate member of the care team with minimum possible delay
- when the client appears to be becoming distressed, immediate reassurance is given by verbal or non-verbal means and consistent with any client beliefs
- where feelings of fear or aggression are expressed, these are treated in a manner which acknowledges the expression as meaningful and important to the client
- the client is given sufficient time, space and privacy to express their distress
- in all cases where the job-holder is unsure of their ability to calm the patient or of the effects that distress may have on the client's condition, appropriate assistance from other care team members is requested

Range: Client groups: all and relating to all personal, cultural and religious beliefs
Care settings: all
Care team: jobholder, professional staff, other supervisors, client, their relavites and friends
Information: is that which is agreed with the care team and is consistent with organisational policy

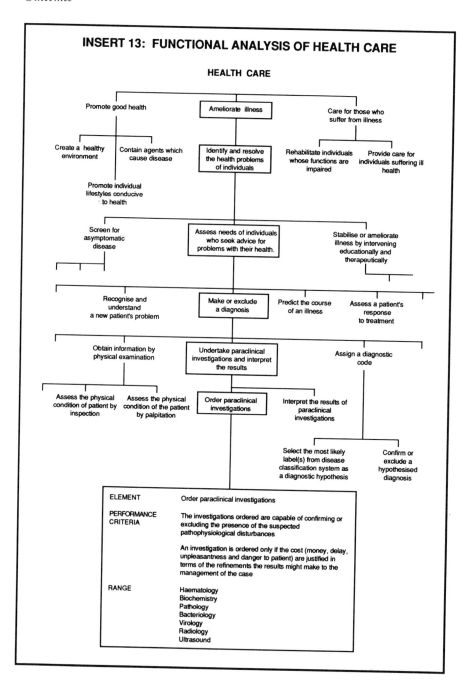

INSERT 13: FUNCTIONAL ANALYSIS OF HEALTH CARE

HEALTH CARE

Promote good health

Ameliorate illness

Care for those who suffer from illness

Create a healthy environment

Contain agents which cause disease

Identify and resolve the health problems of individuals

Rehabilitate individuals whose functions are impaired

Provide care for individuals suffering ill health

Promote individual lifestyles conducive to health

Screen for asymptomatic disease

Assess needs of individuals who seek advice for problems with their health.

Stabilise or ameliorate illness by intervening educationally and therapeutically

Recognise and understand a new patient's problem

Make or exclude a diagnosis

Predict the course of an illness

Assess a patient's response to treatment

Obtain information by physical examination

Undertake paraclinical investigations and interpret the results

Assign a diagnostic code

Assess the physical condition of patient by inspection

Assess the physical condition of the patient by palpitation

Order paraclinical investigations

Interpret the results of paraclinical investigations

Select the most likely label(s) from disease classification system as a diagnostic hypothesis

Confirm or exclude a hypothesised diagnosis

ELEMENT	Order paraclinical investigations
PERFORMANCE CRITERIA	The investigations ordered are capable of confirming or excluding the presence of the suspected pathophysiological disturbances
	An investigation is ordered only if the cost (money, delay, unpleasantness and danger to patient) are justified in terms of the refinements the results might make to the management of the case
RANGE	Haematology Biochemistry Pathology Bacteriology Virology Radiology Ultrasound

may be summarised as follows. First, the key purpose of the overall area of competence is stated; this is then broken down into the primary functions which need to be carried out in order for the key purpose to be achieved. The primary functions are further divided into sub-functions, and they in turn are further sub-divided, and so on.[5] It is easier to understand the process by studying an example as shown in insert 13. The basis on which a function is divided into sub-functions has significant effects on the statements of competence and the form of qualifications and training which result.

The following example of functional analysis, in insert 13, is reproduced from a report by Nick Boreham,[6] who tested the standard setting methodology in medicine, as many people had doubted whether it could be applied to the analysis of competence in professional areas. It represents a personal interpretation of health care and not that of the medical profession.

Summary

The methods for specifying competence, which have evolved over the last six or seven years, are based upon a considerable volume of practical experience. They are being continuously evaluated and refined. The approach differs in several respects from earlier programmes to develop behavioural objectives.[7] First, it is firmly rooted in the functions of employment and focuses on the outcomes required, without imposing an educational model of how people learn and behave. Secondly, it does not limit what is specified in the outcomes by what is considered to be assessable by conventional means. The assumption is made that any outcome that can be clearly articulated can be assessed. The approach to assessment, described in chapter 7, is an integral and essential part of the overall model presented.

6   The Programme to Develop Standards and NVQs

A large programme has grown up over the last few years to set standards (statements of competence) and create NVQs in each occupational area. In the early initiatives, which started in 1986 and 1987, there was limited understanding of how to set about analysing occupational requirements and how to state them in terms of competences. Methods have since been developed and continue to be improved and refined. Good models of statements of competence now exist which are being incorporated into qualifications and training programmes.

Industry Lead Bodies

Within the new arrangements, the standards for qualifications and training are being set by industry, through industry lead bodies. There are currently some 130 lead bodies and a further 20 or so are in the process of being set up. The number will grow as the programme extends to higher professional qualifications, although during the 1990s some merging of bodies will be encouraged to rationalize the standard setting process. Where recognized industry training organizations were already in existence, these bodies have normally been designated as lead bodies for the purpose of setting standards in their sector. Thus all the remaining industry training boards and most of the non-statutory training organizations have taken on this role. Other lead bodies have been created to fill gaps and ensure occupational coverage. Some, such as the new Hairdressing Training Board, have been created as a consortium, representing different factions within the industry. A care sector lead body has brought together a range of professional and trades union interests within health and community care. New lead bodies have been created to represent employment interests in cross-sectoral areas such as clerical and administrative work, which is now covered by the Administrative, Business and Clerical Training Group.

Industry lead bodies are formally recognized or set up by the government's Training Agency. The Training Agency stimulates the setting of standards by funding or contributing to the funding of their development. The TA also provides advice and steers the direction of the projects to varying degrees.[1] Some projects have professional consultants who play a significant role in shaping the standards in consultation with groups of employers and employee representatives. The participation of trades union representatives in the process of setting standards varies from sector to sector. They play a significant role in some lead bodies, such as that in the care sector.

The coverage of occupational areas by lead bodies is untidy and their interests overlap to some degree at the boundaries. The growth of lead bodies from 1986 onwards pre-dated the development of the NVQ framework and any clear conception of how occupations and areas of competence would be classified within the national system.[2] These issues are now being addressed and the framework which is being established will point towards the need for some degree of rationalization of the lead body infrastructure. It will also result in a clearer specification of the area of competence for which each lead body has responsibility.

Problems have been created by trying to develop standards for occupational areas starting from a base of industry training organizations which represent industrial sectors rather than occupations. While many occupations tend to be exclusive to one industry, others might be common to many industries. The situation is even more complex in that the NVQ framework is being designed to rationalize the provision based upon competence defined by employment functions, which are often common to different occupations and different sectors of industry. Competence, occupation and industry are three different forms of classification, which are interrelated in complex ways.

With the recent extension of the NVQ framework to level 5, one can now foresee more professional bodies acting singly or in combination with other professional and industry bodies, participating in the lead bodies network. Some professional bodies are already involved, either setting standards within their own sphere (eg accountancy), or supporting standard setting in occupations for which they have some responsibility (eg dentists participating in the standard setting of dental surgery assistants). The new lead bodies in management, training and development, and information technology are also generating standards which impinge on professional activities at levels 3, 4 and 5 in the NVQ framework. Fortunately, professions tend to be defined in respect to employment function rather than industry and will thus fit more readily into a competence-based framework.

Apart from the lead bodies, referred to above, which are specifying the standards in the occupational areas for which they are responsible, a number of 'generic' lead bodies have been set up to create standards in functional areas which are cross-sectorial. The Administrative, Business and Commercial Training Group provided an early example of a cross-sectorial body.

More recently groups have been set up to cover management and supervision, information technology, training and development and foreign languages. Apart from developing NVQs for people specializing in these areas, it is expected that the units created by these bodies will be adopted widely and incorporated in NVQs, where appropriate, in all occupations. Such centrally devised units clearly offer maximum potential for rationalisation within the NVQ framework.

Awarding Bodies

The other major players in the development and implementation of the new NVQs are the awarding bodies. The term 'awarding body' has been adopted to include examining and validating bodies, and some industry training and professional bodies which award certificates attesting to competence. Currently the established national awarding bodies, such as City and Guilds (C&G), the Royal Society of Arts Examination Board (RSA) and the Business Education and Technical Council (BTEC), are associated with the award of the majority of NVQs. Industry lead bodies frequently enter into a partnership with such national awarding bodies and play a continuing role in the assessment and verification arrangements for the qualification, beyond the setting of standards. For some NVQs the industry lead body takes a primary role in assessment and recording, with the national awarding body providing administrative back up in the issue of certificates. This happens particularly where assessment in the workplace is the primary mode, in which case the industry body may train workplace assessors and supervise the verification arrangements. For other qualifications, the national awarding body assumes almost all responsibility, once the standards have been determined. Some lead bodies, particularly the large industry training boards, act as their own awarding bodies, as do many professional bodies.

Some NVQs are offered by more than one awarding body. This currently happens with the NVQs in Business Administration, which are offered by no less than five bodies. In these circumstances the concept of the NVQ becomes clearer. An NVQ is defined by the statement of competence, and as long as that remains the same there is no reason why different bodies should not offer the same qualification. In fact using the delivery infrastructures of five different awarding bodies results in the Business Administration NVQs being made available to a far larger population than would be possible, at least in the short term, by one body alone. The modes of assessment offered for the same NVQ by the different awarding bodies need not be the same, provided they each provide valid evidence that the same standards have been achieved. In fact, like having more awarding bodies, having a variety of assessment methods (eg workplace observation, competency tests, projects and assignments) opens up the qualification to more people.

Rationalization will be achieved through having only one set of national standards (or statements of competence) in any given occupational area. All awarding bodies offering NVQs in an occupational area will adopt the same standards.

The Development Process

The development process of an NVQ is illustrated in insert 14. The development of standards is partly technical, in that some basic ground rules must be observed in how competence is specified, and partly 'political', in that a consensus and a sense of ownership must be achieved within the occupational area. These two dimensions are intertwined in the development process through successive consultations with larger groups of employers.

INSERT 14: SUMMARY OF THE DEVELOPMENT PROCESS

The primary steps in developing NVQs are:

— determine the area of competence for which NVQs are proposed; map occupational coverage and boundaries;
— identify where the area is located in the NVQ framework and the extent it will overlap and share common areas/units with other sectors and occupations;
— carry out a functional analysis of the area to a level which corresponds to units and elements of competence;
— specify the standards in the form of units of competence, with the constituent elements of competence and performance criteria, range statements, based on the functional analysis;
— circulate draft units and consult widely on their appropriateness and acceptability;
— refine units according to the feedback received from consultations;
— group units into NVQs; negotiate titles, levels, structure with NCVQ to be consistent with its place in the NVQ framework;
— consider arrangements for awarding the NVQs and units;
— if another body is to award the qualification(s), enter into an arrangement with the body at an early stage;
— plan the assessment, recording, verification and certification arrangements while standards are being agreed;
— offer new qualifications in a pilot form during initial period while further refinement and development takes place (this is a common practice with existing qualifications).

(Adapted from Developing NVQs, NCVQ/TA, January, 1990)

The output of a standards development programme is a number of units of competence, the number varying according to size of the area of competence being covered. The units are then grouped into qualifications for inclusion in the NVQ framework. There are a variety of factors to consider in the creation of qualifications.

First, the group of units or employment functions, which make up a qualification must make sense in terms of employment patterns. However, qualifications should not simply reflect the narrow jobs which exist in some industries today.

Second, as qualifications should be designed to set targets for achievement to raise the levels of competence of young people and the workforce as a whole, they must be based upon a concept of future requirements rather than simply reflect current and past practices.

Third, there is the issue of qualifications providing a basis from which one might transfer and progress. They should incorporate in their specification the seeds of future development.

Finally, the 'size' or coverage of a qualification, its relationship to other qualifications, the demands it makes in respect of average time to acquire the qualification in programmes that are subsequently designed for this purpose, and its level in the framework, must be considered. These issues are becoming increasingly important now that targets are being set, schemes are being created and financial vouchers are being allocated, all dependent upon NVQs at particular levels.

Progress to Date

By March 1990, 170 NVQs had been accredited in the NVQ framework which are estimated to cover the employment functions performed by 30 percent of the working population. During the next two to three years the framework will grow rapidly as the products of the standards development programme emerge. By December 1992 it is estimated that there will be nearly 900 NVQs covering the employment functions of up to 80 percent of the working population. The gaps then will be primarily at level 5 and in more specialised areas of employment.[2]

One of the problems with some of the early NVQs created was that they tended to be narrow, focussing on jobs and tasks rather than occupations and functions. That is why considerable stress has been placed upon the need for broader specifications of competence. More recent examples of NVQs, designed according to the methods described in the last few chapters, illustrate the potential of the model.

In conclusion, the fundamental characteristic of the development process is that NVQs should be firmly based upon the needs of employment. But we must also look to the future needs of employment rather than what has been accepted in the past. In doing this, the needs of individuals for broader based training are also likely to be accommodated. One of the major challenges facing those determining training requirements, through the process of creating NVQs, is to incorporate what people currently need to perform their jobs today while preparing them for employment tomorrow. The other feature is the need to involve those in employment as widely as possible in determining or endorsing the competence statements and NVQs. This is not only because they are obviously best placed to know what is required. There is also the important issue of ownership, if industry is to play the major role in training and retraining of the workforce in the future, on the scale which will be required.

7 Assessment

Education and training systems which are outcome-led, such as the NVQ framework and the National Curriculum, require new forms of assessment. Assessment also takes on a more significant role, becoming an integral part of the learning process as well as the means of evaluating it.[1] The introduction of NVQs has seen a reappraisal of traditional examination systems, in which the written essay and, to a lesser extent, multiple-choice tests, have predominated.

Traditional Assessment Practice

Qualifications in general education and in many vocational and professional areas, have traditionally been awarded for success in written examinations at the end of a course or programme. The assessment of skills, except for those which can be tested through writing essays, has tended to contribute very little if anything to the overall result. Skills have not been taken very seriously.[2]

Written examination papers typically allow a choice of questions (for example, 'answer four questions out of 10'), clearly implying a candidate needs to be knowledgeable about only part of the subject covered. The pass mark tends to be set at 50 percent (plus or minus 10 percent), further reducing the knowledge necessary for success. The implication is that it does not matter too much what one knows about a subject or occupation, provided one has a good grasp of some areas of it. Further, certain modes of problem solving ('compare and contrast', 'critically evaluate') and certain forms of presentation (essay writing) are emphasised to the exclusion of others. Thus exams place disproportionate weight on a stylized form of response, sometimes described as examination technique, and in so doing have a serious narrowing effect on education.[3]

Assessment, whether through essay examinations or other means, has been dominated by a psychometric model designed to discriminate between individuals. This model can be seen in its most sophisticated form in the measurement of intelligence and other psychological attributes. The questions chosen and the system of marking adopted, are designed to sort out and grade candidates from best to worst. The pass mark, which embodies the concept of a 'standard' in such assessments, is frequently set to fail a large proportion, sometimes a majority of the candidates. If the candidates improve, year by year, the marking is adjusted to ensure the same proportion fails. The same is true in respect of grades allocated. The proportion of candidates in a subject gaining a first class degree remains much the same year by year, whatever the quality of the candidates. This is known technically as 'norm-referencing', i.e. a mark or grade indicates a candidate's 'ability/attainment' in relation to other candidates. The reference point against which a candidate is marked or graded is how other candidates normally perform. There is no absolute or external standard against which to assess performance.

Within the context of the new model of education and training, these assessment practices seem inappropriate for a variety of reasons.

First, they target education and training on a limited set of goals. If these are not the goals for which the education and training provision is designed, or the assessment only covers part of what is required, then the validity of such assessments must be limited. Validity can only be judged against the outcomes which education and training programmes are perceived to have. If the outcome sought by occupational and professional training, and assessed through qualifications, is to develop competence across a defined range of functions, then norm-referenced assessments of the kind described must be judged to have limited validity.

Second, the traditional practice of loading all the assessment, or almost all, on an examination at the end of the programme must be questioned. Some candidates simply fail and have little to show for their time and effort. There is no record of what they have learnt or what they can do. Qualifications which rely only on end of course assessments are necessarily restricted in what they can cover and ignore a wealth of evidence of the candidates' capabilities which must have been demonstrated throughout the course. In addition, such examination practices place quite unnatural and unnecessary stress on candidates, as we all know. This not only creates a variety of human problems and probably puts many people off education in later life, it also further reduces the validity of assessment by creating artificial conditions in which candidates have to demonstrate their competence. I have often heard people defend this aspect of the examination system, saying that life and work is stressful, and examinations are a good way preparing young people and sorting out those who will be able to cope. I find this argument flawed on various counts. I think we should separate a person's competence in mathematics or engineering from their ability to cope with stress and not let the latter interfere with an assessment of the former. I would also suggest there is very little correlation between coping with examination stress and the sort of stress one encounters in later life. If education and training is about preparing people to cope with adult life and work then it would be more effective to introduce them to the type of problems they will meet rather than creating such artificial contests.[4]

Assessment Based on Specified Outcomes

When the outcomes of learning are clearly specified, as they are in NVQs, assessment must logically be based directly on those outcomes. Statements of competence or attainment lay down what learners are expected to learn, or more precisely what they are expected to be able to do having learnt, and also what should be assessed to confirm that the required learning has been achieved. Outcome based assessment lends itself to continuous assessment rather than end-of-course examinations. It also leads to comprehensive assessment, covering all the outcomes rather than just a sample, and to more emphasis on assessing performance, demonstrations of skill or competence, as well as knowledge.

If we look at the formal requirements for assessment in NVQs as set out by the NVQ criteria we see:

> Assessment may be regarded as the process of collecting evidence and making judgements on whether performance criteria have been met. For the award of an NVQ a candidate must have demonstrated that he or she can meet the performance criteria for each element of competence specified.

(The quotations in this chapter are from 'National Vocational Qualifications: Criteria and Procedures', NCVQ, 1989, unless otherwise stated).

Assessment as Evidence Collection

To look at assessment as evidence collection helps one recognise that formal examinations and tests provide only one form of evidence. Other, and more natural sources of evidence can be found in performance at work or outside. For many who have viewed assessment for qualifications as inseparable from the formal instruments of assessment (examinations and tests), this is a major conceptual change.

In systems of education and training where standards of performance are not independently defined, the only concept of a standard is that which is defined by, and imbedded within, the exams or tests set. Assessment is then inevitably tied to such exams and tests. But once standards are set out independently of assessment, as in NVQs, it creates opportunities for different forms of assessment. Instead of allowing the assessment to define the standards, the standards now define what needs to be assessed.

There are two processes involved in assessment:

— the collection of evidence;
— making judgements on whether the evidence meets the standards, which in NVQs means whether the performance criteria for an element have been met.

This introduces another consideration of the sufficiency of evidence required to make the decision that the candidate is competent. It raises such questions as, how many demonstrations do we need to see? Do we need to check knowledge and understanding as well as see the candidate perform?

Before we leave the above criterion, it should be noted that each element of competence must be assessed in an NVQ. This is in marked contrast to the practices of sampling, allowing a choice of questions, and 50 percent pass marks that are common in traditional qualifications. Comprehensive assessment is a logical requirement if we wish to ensure that a candidate is competent in those functions listed in a statement of competence. The National Curriculum is moving in a similar direction, requiring assessment in respect of all 'statements of attainment' (see chapter 10).

Emphasis on Performance

Another NVQ criterion to note is:

Performance must be demonstrated and assessed under conditions as close as possible to those under which it would normally be practised.

Performance demonstrations must provide the evidence, or at least part of the evidence, required to assess competence. It is important to recognise that competence often depends on being able to cope with a range of contextual factors which go beyond the performance of the task in hand. That is why demonstrations in context, or simulations which replicate the important contextual factors, are considered requirements of assessment. For example, it means a shift away from the artificiality of many tests of competence or skill that have been common in the past to making assessment more realistic. This is one reason why there has been a growth in workplace assessment to meet the requirements of NVQs.

NVQ criteria do not, however, specify the method of assessment, because one of the objectives is to open access to assessment to as many people as possible. NVQs do, of course,

... require the method of assessment used in any circumstance to be appropriate, relevant, valid and reliable ...

The new model of assessment requires a re-evaluation of the concepts of validity and reliability. It certainly raises questions about the traditional emphasis placed upon reliability of assessments. An earlier note on this issue reproduced at Appendix D, suggests that validity is the objective of assessment, while reliability, is important only in so far as it contributes to valid assessment decisions. There are circumstances in which attempts to increase reliability reduce validity.[5]

Validity, in NVQs is achieved by:

— making clear statements of what is to be assessed, as provided by the elements of competence, performance criteria and range statements;
— collecting or generating evidence that relates directly to the activity described by the element;
— ensuring that the evidence meets the performance criteria, and;
— ensuring the evidence is sufficient.

Modes of Assessment

The elements of competence and performance criteria indicate the form of evidence required. As we have seen earlier an element of competence should consist of an active verb, an object and the conditions under which the competence is practised. Taking an example from the NVQ in pensions administration and the unit 'establish and maintain member and scheme records', we have:

Element of competence:

'create	records (manual or computer)	for new members'
(active verb)	(object)	(conditions)

Performance criteria:

— record is checked after entry to confirm accuracy
— record does conform with information submitted and details calculated
— record follows employer's conventions (eg surname first, leading zeros used, accepted abbreviations used)

The active verb, together with the performance criteria, indicate the form of evidence required and the modes of assessment which are possible. 'Create records' requires an activity to be performed and the performance criteria point to the need for some degree of observation of that activity by an assessor and an inspection of the output — the record. This could be done in the workplace, the context in which it will normally be performed. It would also appear that this element could also be faithfully simulated in a college or training centre, if office conditions are created.

Workplace Assessment

As a general rule, assessment of performance in the course of normal work offers the most natural form of evidence of competence and has several advantages, both technical and economic. The term 'normal work' needs some explanation. It can include being a full-time paid employee or it could mean being a trainee carrying out the functions normally performed by an employee in a work placement. The essential characteristic is not the status of the person being assessed but that the performance of the employment functions is for 'real', in that the person deals with customers, clients or patients, and handles equipment, instruments and materials, in the contexts and conditions that normally pertain to employment in the occupation.

The conditions of assessment should reflect all aspects of the conditions of work as far as is possible. Work conditions are varied and complex and may include a number of the following: — time pressures, a number of tasks to perform simultaneously or successively, conflicting demands, machinery, tools, equipment and materials, confidentiality, security, hazards, space, weather, patterns of inter-relationship etc. Obviously assessment in ongoing work is likely to include some of these conditions, as the assessment actually takes place under the normal demands of work and in a work environment.

Multiple assessment, showing that an individual can perform in a range of circumstances representing the variation which occurs naturally in the work environment, provides the most satisfactory evidence of occupational competence. Artificially limiting the conditions of the assessment situation in order to standardize performance and increase reliability, may have unacceptable consequences on the validity of assessment.

There are, of course, well established practices of workplace assessment in certain professional areas such as medicine, dentistry, teaching and flying aeroplanes. There are some activities where there is obviously no substitute for learning by doing the job, normally under close supervision at first, and assessment to ensure that the trainee can do it. In many other areas work experience forms part of the training, or a probationary period of employment after formal training is required for qualification in an occupation or profession. But frequently, such work experience is neither properly structured nor assessed.

There is now a growing body of evidence to show that assessment can be carried out in the workplace by managers and supervisors, when performance is judged against elements of competence.[6] One of the earliest examples was in the area of catering, where the Hotel and Catering Training Board introduced CATERBASE, a unit based system of accreditation in 1986. CATERBASE has been extensively evaluated. The units are now part of a number of NVQs which are certificated by City & Guilds. Similar systems have since been introduced in a wide variety of industries, including clothing manufacture, retail distribution, business administration, pensions management, marine engineering and many others.

Workplace assessment of NVQs is conducted with a degree of formality, made possible by the explicit standards of performance provided by elements and performance criteria. This brings a rigour to assessment which has seldom been present in workplace assessment in the past. Without agreement on the standards by which people are judged, workplace assessment, or any form of assessment, will be highly subjective.[7]

The requirements of workplace assessment for NVQs are that companies (or more generally employing organisations) are approved by awarding bodies as local assessment centres for the purpose of awarding a qualification or set of qualifications. Small employers may be part of a larger consortium which acts collectively as an assessment centre. To be approved the company/consortium must fulfil certain criteria which normally include having trained (competent) assessors, internal verifiers (ie people to check that assessment is being carried out according to requirements) and procedures for recording assessments, maintaining records and conveying the information to the awarding body. In addition, representatives of the awarding body will also visit the centres from time to time to check assessment and recording practices. The procedures are in fact the same as apply to colleges and training centres which act as local assessment centres, of which there is much experience.

The key person in all this is the assessor who must normally be in day to day contact with the trainee or employee being assessed. In most situations this can only be the first line supervisor. Along with the role of assessor usually goes that of trainer. One should not underestimate the demands this places on supervisors, but there is encouraging evidence from YTS and now NVQs, that they are well able to respond if given appropriate support. These issues are considered as part of the general implications for employers of the new model of education and training at chapter 13.

The potential benefits of making supervisors and managers responsible for assessment and continuing learning are considerable. A consciousness of the standards required in their employment area relates closely to their primary role of maintaining standards of performance and quality of products and services in their company. It provides a framework and a language to discuss improving their company standards and the quality of their products. As trainers, managers and supervisors will be expected to set an example by their own adherence to standards.

The credibility of assessment at work still needs to be established despite considerable progress made in the last four years.[6] The belief that it refers to the rather casual and subjective practices that have prevailed in the past is still widespread. Even those who understand something of recent developments, doubt whether supervisors can or will be objective in their assessment of trainees and employees, although the situation is not so different from that of teachers and lecturers assessing their students, a practice which has been accepted.

The openness of the process, with assessors and employees all knowing the standards by which performance is judged, will help to deter bad practice. At least it will be difficult to hide it. Some early evidence from evaluation studies in catering suggest that supervisors were conscientious, tending to err on the side of requiring too much evidence rather than too little. Some supervisors clearly wished to protect standards in their occupation and were careful about endorsing the competence of new entrants. Some were concerned about their reputation among colleagues if they were too lenient. If a company or occupation recognizes a collective responsibility to uphold standards, then assessment is likely to be carried out rigorously. Taking assessment at work seriously is part of a change in culture that is required in companies if continuing learning is to become a reality.

To cover all the occupational activities required by an NVQ, opportunities for learning and assessment will often need to extend beyond an employee's own job or a single work experience placement. These can be provided by job enlargement, temporary redeployment in other sections, possibly even providing experience in a second plant or company. NVQs are designed not only to ensure training to high standards but also extending the range of competence of employees.

In addition to normal work experience, employees or trainees may also undertake projects and assignments to extend their experience and opportunities for assessment. YTS and other workbased training programmes have illustrated what is possible.

When the possibilities of learning and assessment at work are exhausted, one must look outside to what colleges and training centres or open learning materials can provide. The assessment of competence outside the workplace means recreating the essential characteristics of the employment functions through simulation.

Although, assessment at work is normally assumed to refer to paid employment, the principles outlined obviously apply equally to unpaid work in the voluntary sector or in the home. The only constraints are simply practical issues of how evidence of competence generated in more private contexts can be gathered for assessors to make judgements. Where products or records are produced which can attest to competence then it becomes feasible. The next chapter on the accreditation of prior learning provides some examples of how this might be achieved.

Simulation of Employment Functions

If trainees are attending a college or training centre, the obvious, and normally the most economical mode of assessment, is to collect evidence of their performance continuously throughout the training period. If people are practising to develop skills, as they would need to during training, they are also providing a potential source of evidence for the assessment of those skills. This could take place in a training workshop where, say, engineering or construction skills are being practised, in a college restaurant training caterers, in a model office where trainees are practising clerical skills, and so on. If such programmes are designed to meet the standards specified in NVQs, the activities, projects and assignments which provide the vehicles for practice and learning, can be designed to yield evidence for assessment.

The extent to which simulated employment activity in training workshops and colleges can encompass the essential characteristics of the workplace is debatable and the subject of current research. The introduction of NVQs has certainly encouraged many colleges to create more realistic training and assessment environments in an attempt to reflect work practice.

Outside of training workshops, similar approaches can be used in the classroom. Increasingly, programmes are being designed in the form of a series of activities, projects or assignments, to encourage more active participation in learning, through individual or group activity. While such activities are designed primarily as vehicles for learning, they can also be used for assessment. Assessment will focus learners more systematically on the objectives they are trying to achieve and the feedback they receive from the evaluation of their performance will facilitate learning.

If the evidence of performance required for assessment cannot be derived, or not fully derived, from work or training activity, then the alternative is some form of set piece test of a more conventional kind.

Competency Testing

The development of competency testing builds upon a range of experience in what have variously been described as skills tests, achievement tests, proficiency tests and so on. They may vary in length from 15 to 30 minutes for testing typing and driving, to two or three days for tests in the construction industry. There will certainly a be role for such testing, both to supplement workplace assessment and continuous assessment in training, and as an alternative for people who do not have access to the workplace or training programmes. There is also the need to assess and accredit those who are already competent by virtue of their past experience. This issue is considered in the next chapter on the accreditation of prior learning.

Competency tests have some technical advantages in that the task or activity to be assessed, and the conditions under which it is carried out, can

---

INSERT 15: OPEN ACCESS TO ASSESSMENT

A principle of the new model of education and training is that there should be open access to assessment and accreditation. This implies making it possible for people to be assessed by whatever valid modes are available. In an ideal world, each NVQ and unit of competence should be on offer both for assessment in the workplace, assessment in colleges and training centres and assessment through competency tests. This would maximise opportunity. There would also be a whole range of related programmes and learning support 'materials to help individuals become competent via different routes. Economic, practical and technical constraints are likely to prevent this being fully realised, but wherever feasible, alternative modes of assessment should be promoted.

---

be controlled, which should produce more reliable results. However, the greater control and reliability is achieved by limiting the range of variables that can be tested. Competency tests are often perceived as lacking the reality of work, because they tend to isolate and test certain skills while neglecting others.

It is difficult to generalize about the validity of competency tests. The essential characteristics of some employment functions can be encapsulated in a controlled test while others certainly cannot. The expense of attempting to simulate some employment functions would be prohibitive. Other functions which draw upon interpersonal and group performance, a common feature at higher levels, do not lend themselves to such testing.

The fact that NVQs, and other outcome-led systems of learning, are moving towards more comprehensive forms of assessment covering all the outcomes, makes competency testing less practicable than continuous assessment. To cover all the elements within an NVQ may require a battery of tests, taking days to administer at considerable cost. But again it is not possible to generalize. In some occupational areas a large number of elements of competence can all be demonstrated in one integrated activity. It would not take long to assess the competence of a professional tennis player. Even less a professional sprinter. Where occupational competence depends on a highly developed but limited skill, testing is easier than in those occupations which require a wide range of diverse skills and knowledge.

To conclude this brief resumé of performance assessment methods, it is suggested that assessment should, wherever possible, take advantage of evidence generated in the course of employment, training or other activities. Such evidence will normally be more realistic, more diverse and less costly to collect. The alternative is to create situations specifically for assessment in the form of a test.

Continuous assessment at work or during training offers a wealth of evidence over time, often several demonstrations of each element, which is not possible in tests where time is severely limited. Workplace assessment scores high on realism as it is comes closest to the behaviour one is trying to assess. It suffers in the degree of control that can be exercised over situations, for assessors often have to observe what occurs naturally rather than constructing the situations to order. This is both the strength and the weakness of workbase assessment.

INSERT 16: INSUFFICIENT EVIDENCE?

The Final Report of the Competency Testing Project
by Lindsay Mitchell and Tommy Cuthbert, SCOTVEC, 1989

By far the most extensive review of competency testing practice in the UK is contained in the above report. Twenty one different schemes were evaluated against the NVQ criteria and the report concluded: 'Very few of the assessment systems currently available assess all aspects of the competence upon which they are based, with only a sample of competence assessed and inference made across to all aspects ... Many systems appear to have sacrificed validity in favour of standardization ... There must be considerable doubt as to whether any, or many, of the current competency tests actually gain sufficient evidence for inferences of competence to be made.'

The creation of test situations in the workplace combines some of the advantages of the workplace with the control that can be exercised in tests. These have been described as 'extracted samples of work'. This method is used to assess tractor driving in an NVQ in agriculture. A test situation is created in which the candidate completes specified manoeuvres, but the test takes place at the candidate's normal place of work and uses the tractor the candidate would normally use. In this example an external assessor visits the farm to check performance but this need not always be so. There is clearly much scope for employees or trainees in the workplace to carry out predetermined activities ('set-pieces'), in their normal place of work. This could usefully supplement continuous assessment at work.

Supplementary Evidence

The evidence of competence that can be collected through performance demonstrations will not normally be sufficient to confirm that a candidate is fully competent in the range of situations in which he or she might be expected to practise. The range statement, which is now normally added to an element of competence, indicates the range of contexts to which the element applies. (See description and examples in chapter 5.)

It would clearly be impossible to assess candidates in all the situations in which they might, in the future, be expected to perform. A judgement therefore has to be made as to whether candidates, who have demonstrated that they can perform to set standards in one situation, can transfer their skills to others. If variation in practice is small, then it might be reasonable to assume they can. In the driving test, a demonstration that a person can drive one car under certain conditions to the required standard, is sufficient to certificate them to drive any car under any conditions. But in other areas we need confirmation that the candidate is able to cope with the variation in practice required for different patients, customers, equipment and so on.

Competent performance is underpinned by skills and knowledge. To ensure that people will be able to adapt to different and varied situations where their performance has not been demonstrated, the best we can do is to check that they understand the general principles which underly their task and how their performance should be modified to meet changing circumstances. For high level competences the body of knowledge and theory which underpins competence may be considerable. These issues are considered in greater detail in chapter 18, as the role of knowledge in a competence-based system of education and training is a major subject of debate. It is sufficient in this chapter to recognize that the assessment of competence for NVQs requires demonstrations in at least one context and will normally require supplementary evidence from the assessment of knowledge and sometimes skill. Knowledge is assessed through oral or written questioning, or through the presentation of a problem which tests the application of knowledge. It is considered important for NVQs that the assessment of knowledge is closely related to its application. Oral questioning which takes place during or following demonstrations in the workplace or college would seem to be the most natural. Like performance assessment, it could form an integral part of the learning process in which learners were encouraged to think about 'why' they needed to perform in a certain way and 'what if' the circumstances were different.

Evidence arising from previous experience may contribute to the assessment. A portfolio of art or design work might for instance be submitted, allowing prior achievement to be accredited. The 'accreditation of prior learning' is likely to become a major feature of assessment for NVQs as more experienced adults participate in vocational training. As this issue always arouses considerable interest it is considered more fully in the next chapter.

The primary methods of assessment are shown in insert 17. They may be classified according to whether they collect evidence of performance (ie doing something) or supplementary evidence normally of knowledge and understanding. The distinction is not clear cut in that some knowledge and understanding can be inferred from performance, while written and oral responses may tap some aspects of performance.

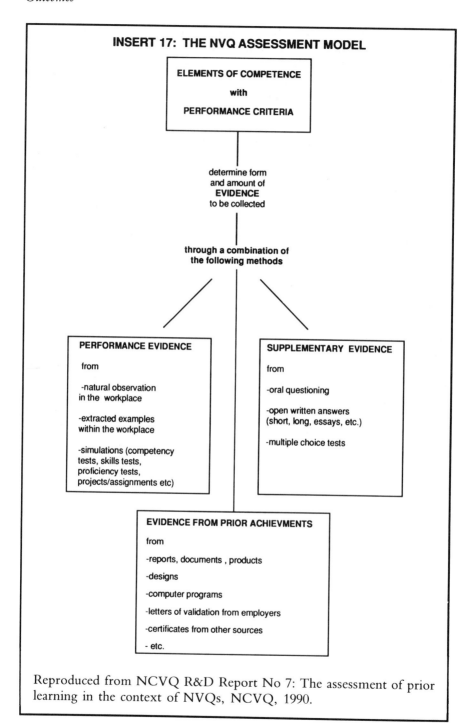

INSERT 17: THE NVQ ASSESSMENT MODEL

ELEMENTS OF COMPETENCE

with

PERFORMANCE CRITERIA

determine form
and amount of
EVIDENCE
to be collected

**through a combination of
the following methods**

PERFORMANCE EVIDENCE

from

-natural observation
in the workplace

-extracted examples
within the workplace

-simulations (competency
tests, skills tests,
proficiency tests,
projects/assignments etc)

SUPPLEMENTARY EVIDENCE

from

-oral questioning

-open written answers
(short, long, essays, etc.)

-multiple choice tests

EVIDENCE FROM PRIOR ACHIEVMENTS

from

-reports, documents , products

-designs

-computer programs

-letters of validation from employers

-certificates from other sources

- etc.

Reproduced from NCVQ R&D Report No 7: The assessment of prior learning in the context of NVQs, NCVQ, 1990.

It is important to note that the mode or modes of assessment chosen should not place unnecessary additional demands which may inhibit or prevent a candidate from demonstrating what they can do or what they know or understand. This is most likely to happen in the assessment of knowledge and understanding using written tests. Having to read and interpret questions and then record their response, often demands intellectual and communication competences which go beyond those required to carry out the activity being assessed. It is commonly recognized that 'coping with exams' is a skill in itself having little or nothing to do with the content of the examinations. The introduction of these additional demands, apart from being unfair, can only reduce the validity of the assessment method.

The above issue is especially pertinent to candidates who are disabled or have special needs. The mode of assessment can unwittingly debar or disadvantage the blind or the deaf, for example, when they might be perfectly capable of carrying out the function if alternative modes were provided. If a candidate can meet the performance criteria with the use of special aids, such as those they could use when employed, then their use in assessment is quite legitimate. The open access policy for NVQs, plus the unit credit system which recognises separate competences and the accreditation of prior learning, all have particular advantages in recognising the competence of those with special needs.

In summary, assessment is demystified in the NVQ model. The outcomes are clearly stated and the standards by which they are assessed are made quite explicit. In addition, assessment is regarded as a natural process of gathering evidence, most often from everyday life and work. As we shall see in the next chapter this can also include evidence from past experience.

8   The Accreditation of Prior Learning

For some years researchers have struggled to find a way of giving credit for people's past achievements within traditional qualification systems. The accreditation of prior learning — APL, as it is commonly known — can now be realised as a natural part of the NVQ model. As we have seen in the last chapter, assessment in NVQs is a matter of collecting evidence from any relevant source, and a person's past achievements are one potential source. Unlike most traditional qualifications, the award of an NVQ is based solely on the assessment of competence and is not concerned about how such competence is acquired. Learning from experience and presenting evidence of competence from such experience becomes a legitimate route to qualifications. This chapter looks at how it can be built into the NVQ model.

In the past, the problem with accrediting prior learning has been how to relate an individual's competence, as demonstrated through past experience, to the standards required by qualifications. If the standards are not stated separately from the assessment instruments, it is not technically possible. Trying to relate work experience to the requirements of written examinations and multiple choice tests is hardly feasible. As the standards for NVQs are made quite explicit in statements of competence this problem is removed.[1] In addition, as the standards relate directly to employment, they can be understood and recognized by those with experience in the appropriate field.

The Requirements for APL

If the accreditation of prior learning is to become a practical proposition, a number of conditions must be met. The qualifications must:

— allow open access to assessment, independent of mode of learning, programme or course;
— allow assessment which accepts any form of valid evidence;

— spell out what is assessed for the award of the qualification (i.e. state the outcomes required in the form of statements of competence or attainment);

— allow credit for part achievement of qualifications (i.e. have some form of unit/modular credit arrangements).

NVQs have all these characteristics. In addition, arrangements must be in place for:

— the widespread provision of local assessment centres approved by awarding bodies;

— information, guidance and support to candidates who wish to submit evidence of prior achievements;

— a process by which an individual's experience and achievements can be matched against the requirements of the qualifications — the statements of competence or attainment;

— a means of collecting evidence of past achievements (demonstrations of competence). This is carried out mostly by the candidate with guidance from assessors;

— a process by which assessors examine the evidence submitted to see if it meets the standards required (the performance criteria in NVQs) and is sufficient. Questioning the candidate to confirm authenticity of the evidence and collecting supplementary evidence is part of this process;

— a process of assessing candidates at the time of application (competency testing) in areas where they claim to be competent, but cannot supply satisfactory evidence;

The last item recognizes that, evidence of past experience and achievements, often needs to be supplemented by current assessments to fill in gaps and extend the evidence provided. The award of unit credits or qualifications to candidates undergoing APL is normally based on a mixture of evidence from different sources.

Given the NVQ model, the accreditation of prior learning is no longer a conceptual or technical problem, but there are still a variety of practical issues to be resolved. The first is, can candidates actually supply appropriate evidence?

The programme referred to in insert 18 provided valuable experience. It showed that with a little imagination candidates were able to collect various forms of evidence which went at least part of the way to confirming their competence. Some of the categories of evidence supplied are shown in insert 19.

The evidence can take the form of products or artifacts (written reports, designs, computer programmes, machine tools, manufactured products etc.), documentation (job descriptions, production schedules, accounts etc.) or endorsements of performance (previous certificates, letters of validation,

---

INSERT 18: THE TA/NCVQ NATIONAL APL PROGRAMME[2]

A national programme to test the feasibility of APL in colleges of further education and training centres has recently been completed.[1] Its objective was to develop and test a model of the accreditation of prior learning which, if successful, would be adopted by awarding bodies as part of their normal assessment and certification practice. A feature of the programme was the active participation of the main national awarding bodies, City & Guilds, BTEC and the RSA Examination Board plus one industry awarding body, the Hotel and Catering Training Board.

Its objective was largely achieved. APL was introduced on a limited scale at five colleges of further education and one skill centre. It proved to be feasible, if time consuming, to collect evidence and assess the competence of clients against the standards required for the award of unit credits and qualifications. The awarding bodies monitored and applied their normal standards of verification to the local assessments and were satisfied that the evidence of competence collected was sufficient to meet, and sometimes exceeded, their quality control requirements. The study concluded that APL is feasible and could be highly cost-effective if it were introduced as part of the new model of vocational education and training based on NVQs.

---

photographs etc.). On the last issue it is possible to go back to employers and check details of past performance against NVQ requirements. This may be viewed as 'retrospective' workplace assessment.

The use of evidence from prior achievements, supplemented by current assessments, is perhaps best appreciated from case studies from the project as shown in insert 20.

If the accreditation of prior learning is introduced as a general feature of education and training in the future, it will need to be part of a wider service. We have seen already that evidence from prior experience needs to be supplemented by current assessments, so these facilities should be in place. There is a need for good information of what is on offer in the qualification system that might be relevant to a candidate's experience. There is the need for guidance to help candidates review their past experience and identify what competences they possess. There is a tendency for people to under-estimate what they can do and the value of their experience, especially if their skills have not been acquired in formal training. Some candidates need counselling to build up their confidence before they can recognise that they have skills worth accrediting.

APL normally leads to some unit credits and partial qualification. It also indicates additional competences, partially acquired, which fall short of the

INSERT 19: SUMMARY OF EVIDENCE

What follows is a summary of some of the evidence provided by candidates during the project by qualification. In addition to the evidence they submitted, almost all candidates underwent some form of oral questioning, demonstration, simulation, assignment, observation in the work place and/or written testing.

BTEC NATIONAL CERT. IN BUS. STUDIES
Computer print outs and disks, income and expenditure accounts, invoices, statements, cash flow forecasts, budget control statements, letters of validation from employers, previous certificates.

BTEC NATIONAL DIPLOMA IN COMPUTING
Computer print-outs, letters of validation from employers.

C&G 201 IN ENGINEERING
Components operations schedule, bench work, previous certificates, letter of validation from employers.

RSA DOP AND CLAIT
Photocopies of petty cash wages and other documents related to the qualification, previous certificates, letters of validation from employers.

BTEC HIGHER DIPLOMA IN ENGINEERING
Job descriptions, production schedules, letters of validation from employers.

C&G 706/1 IN CATERING
Menus, photographs, industrial awards, medals, previous certificates, letters of validation from employers.

C&G 383 IN MOTOR VEHICLE MAINTENANCE
Rally car (brought to centre) photographs, previous certificates, letters of validation from employers.

standards required. As a consequence candidates often need some further training or experience in specific areas to acquire a full qualification. This immediately raises the need for a programme of learning tailored to meet the needs of the candidate. Unless this can be supplied, the advantages of APL will be severely limited.

For these reasons APL should be seen as an integral part of the new model of education and training and not pursued in isolation. Chapter 12,

INSERT 20: CASE STUDIES FROM THE NCVQ/TA APL
PROGRAMME

(from NCVQ R&D Report No. 7, Accreditation of Prior Learning
in the context of National Vocational Qualifications)

Case Study 1, Maureen, Filton Technical College

Maureen is 35, married with two sons aged 18 and 16. She left school in
1969 with two GCE O levels and one CSE grade 1. At 31 she gained a
good range of RSA and Pitman secretarial qualifications. Since entering
full-time employment, Maureen has had a variety of jobs; but for the
past 5 years she has worked as an Administration Officer with the
Ministry of Defence. On hearing about the APL service at Filton,
Maureen decided to apply for credits in BTEC National and Business
Studies. She was asked to review the Elements of Competence indicat-
ing whether or not she believed that she had the stated competence
and, if so, to indicate how she could prove it. This self-assessment was
completed as part of the initial screening phase of the process.

The candidate then began collecting the necessary evidence to
prove her claim to competence and prepare for the assessment process
itself.

The assessment then took place with reference to each element of
competence. The candidate was expected to satisfy all of the performance criteria under each and did so in a variety of ways. For example,
Element of Competence 2, 'create a spreadsheet on commercially
available software', was assessed by scrutiny of a letter of validation,
a simulation exercise performed in front of the assessor, and oral
questioning.

Case Study 2, Pearl, Crosskeys College of Further Education[3]

Pearl, a woman of 42 years, had left school at 15, worked as an assistant
in a grocery and provisions store; married and had a family. In 1976 she
began part-time employment as a vending service operator. Since join-
ing this company she had many different promotions including assistant
cook, control manager and manager. In 1980 in addition to her employment, Pearl started a small outside catering business producing food for
wedding receptions, buffets and private parties. She approached the
college seeking accreditation for the catering qualification C&G 706/1
and enrolled as a part-time student for the the higher level, C&G 706/2.

Pearl claimed credit for and was assessed for all units in the 706/1 and,
with a little top-up, was recommended for the entire qualification. This
included units in industrial studies, observing safe practices, observing
safe hygiene practices and basic preparatory tasks; also boiling, poach-

ing, stewing, braising, steaming, baking, roasting, grilling, shallow frying, deep frying, micro wave cookery, cold preparations, catering and food science and catering and business calculations. Her assessments were based on a wide range of evidence from photographs, menus, a letter of validation from her employer, telephone discussions between the employer and the assessor, oral questioning and for all units the knowledge-based short answer C&G tests, all of which Pearl passed at her first attempt. Further instruction for the units in safe practices and safe hygiene practices was provided by the HCTB Mastercraft Series Videos and Food Craftbook, before their accreditation.

Case Study 3, Veronica, Blackpool and the Fylde College

Veronica is in her mid-forties and has been separated from her husband for the last five years. She has two teenage children. She left school with her GCEs and over the years has had a number of part-time and full-time jobs. She has responsibility for completing wages administration, assistance with accounts and the more general administrative support. She came to Blackpool and the Fylde College seeking certification for the RSA Diploma in Office Procedures (DOP). For her assessment she needed to prove her competence in the 20 different tasks specified by the qualification. She successfully did this in a variety of ways:

1 Detailed letters from her employers were submitted.
2 Previous certificates were evaluated.
3 She submitted copies of her petty cash, wages and other documented records.
4 She was observed in a number of different workshops (simulations)
5 She received further training at the college.

Case Study 4, Kevin, Newport College of Further Education[3]

Kevin is 40, married with two children. He has been employed by the same company for 20 years and has progressed to his current position as shift foreman on the production process. One of his main duties in this post is that of site safety officer. In spite of his long tenure with the firm, Kevin felt vunerable to redundancy because he lacked qualifications. According to the assessor, Kevin appeared to lack confidence in spite of his obvious experience and competence.

He presented himself for the C&G201 in engineering. Kevin sought accreditation in nine 201 units and underwent a wide variety of assessment processes. For example, his employer verified that Kevin was competent in hard and soft soldering, brazing, electric arc welding, oxy-acetylene gas welding, mig welding, foe butt, lap and fillet welding.

In addition, the letter confirmed Kevin's ability to use a wide variety of tools, instruments and equipment. Even with this detailed letter, the candidate was asked to demonstrate a number of his claimed competences and in one instance participated in a simulation exercise to prove his competence in 'moving loads'. The candidate also successfully completed the C&G knowledge tests, as required.

The college staff hope that since his success with the 201, Kevin will attempt some of the BTEC National Diploma in Engineering units.

which pulls together the various strands of the model, shows how APL fits in.

The NVQ Database

One aspect of the new model, which has particular relevance to APL, is the NVQ database.[3] The NVQ framework is now available on a computer database with each NVQ, broken down into units and elements of competence, plus performance criteria and range statements, accessible on a personal computer. During the transitional phase while the NVQ framework builds up, the database also contains information on all the other vocational qualifications offered by the main national awarding bodies. The database will play a very significant role in APL in the future, as well as providing information for guidance and action planning.

APL candidates will be able to explore the occupational areas in which they claim competence. Starting from a menu of the broad areas of competence (e.g. catering, agriculture), they can rapidly home in through successive menus to those specific functions in which they have experience. They can directly match their experience against the elements of competence, checking to see if they believe they can perform to the standards indicated by the performance criteria. This process will normally be mediated by a counsellor, but given user friendly software, many candidates will be able to interact directly with the database.

Through the above process, a profile could be generated by the candidate of the units and elements in which they claim to be competent. Evidence would then be collected, in so far as it was possible, to substantiate the claim. An assessor would examine the evidence and judge its validity and sufficiency for the award of the units. In the future more sophisticated software should make it possible to carry out some of the assessment and the checking of evidence through questioning the candidate via the computer.

The NCVQ database also has an important role in action planning. Having gained credit for a range of units through APL, or from previous certification, if these units are fed into the computer, it will be able to inform users of all the qualifications which contain some or all of the units. Discussions are also proceeding on linking the qualification database to those which provide information on learning opportunities, such as Training Access Points (TAPS). Having once decided what units an individual wants to pursue, information can then be obtained on what courses, programmes, open learning materials, work experience placements, and so on, are available to help. The full potential of the database and associated systems will only be realised when the NVQ framework is fully developed and all qualifications are in units which can be separately assessed.

Summary

The accreditation of prior learning will have an important role in the future as more adults participate in education and training. APL is particularly relevant to people returning to work or changing careers. NVQs have been designed to increase access to qualifications through APL and by other means. Recent research has demonstrated the feasibility of APL and the participation of the national awarding bodies in the programme has convinced them that it can be built into their assessment and verification procedures. But APL will only make sense if incorporated as part of a comprehensive provision of assessment and learning opportunities, that is, as part of the model presented in this book.

9 Credit Accumulation and Transfer

A characteristic of competence-based qualifications such as NVQs, and more generally any system which is outcome-led such as the National Curriculum, is the assessment and accreditation of smaller 'chunks' of programmes or syllabuses than occur in traditional qualifications. Once the outcomes of learning are spelled out, and assessment is based upon those outcomes, then credit can be awarded for individual outcomes. This drives education and training towards unit-credit systems or 'profiles' of attainment, which in turn leads to modular programmes of learning. Unit accreditation offers many advantages which are considered in this chapter.

Within NVQs, each element of competence is assessed. This would make it possible to award credit for the achievement of elements, but this option was not chosen. It was considered that elements would be too small for separate credit and would provide too much detailed information for users to handle. Further, elements often do not stand as independent achievements, separate from the unit of which they are a constituent part. It was therefore decided that units of competence were a more appropriate size for the formal award of credit.

Units of competence should be designed with this consideration in mind. They should represent a discrete function or activity in employment which is recognisable to employers and employees. Competence in the function should also be perceived to have value by making the holder of a unit-credit more employable.

Given the way work is structured, units are likely to be larger (i.e. take longer to achieve) as one moves up the levels of the NVQ framework. Units also provide targets for learning, and the possibility of achieving them within a reasonable time scale has a positive motivating effect on the learner. However, to provide such motivation, units have got to be worth achieving. To create the most appropriate units of competence in an occupational or professional area, it will be evident that a number of factors must be taken into account and a balance achieved between them.

For these reasons NCVQ does not prescribe the 'size' of a unit or the

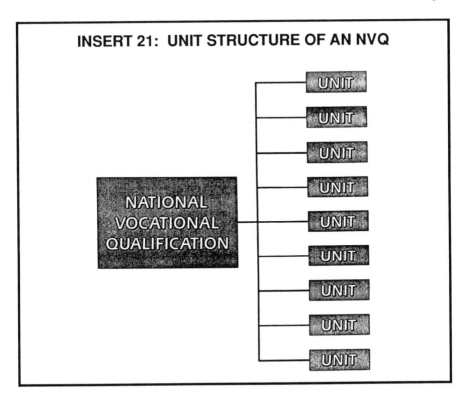

INSERT 21: UNIT STRUCTURE OF AN NVQ

number of units in an NVQ. It varies according to the functional breakdown of occupations and level. The number of units in an NVQ tends to be between 5 and 20.

The advantages of unit accreditation may be summarized as:

— credit may be awarded for relatively small achievements which might otherwise go unrecognised;
— achievements in programmes can be formally recognised even though the programme is not completed;
— if units are common to different qualifications and programmes, it allows credit transfer which avoids unnecessary repetition in learning;
— it allows access to learning and achievement of just those units required by an individual without the necessity of undergoing the requirements of a full qualification;
— it provides short term targets which have a positive motivating effect on the learner;[1]
— it allows credits for achievements from different modes of learning, in different locations (eg the workplace, college, open learning) to be accumulated within the same system for the award of a qualification;
— it provides more informative certification of achievements;

The National System of Credit Accumulation and Transfer

In 1988, the National Council for Vocational Qualifications launched a national system of credit accumulation and transfer.[2] Fourteen awarding bodies were initially invited to join and all accepted. They included the major bodies such as the City and Guilds, BTEC, RSA Examinations Board, LCCI and Pitmans. All the awarding bodies agreed to restructure their qualifications in unit form, where necessary, and to offer the units for separate assessment. They further agreed to recognise the units of the other awarding bodies as credits towards their own qualifications where the units were common.

The move towards unit based accreditation normally implies local assessment at centres approved by the awarding bodies and continuous assessment during programmes, rather than assessment of the whole programme at the end. It also requires awarding bodies to verify assessments at unit level, recording the successful outcomes centrally and awarding certificates (sometimes called Records of Achievement) to candidates in respect of the units achieved. These constituted major changes in practice for some awarding bodies and at the time of writing (June, 1990), the transition has only been partially achieved.

The National Record of Vocational Achievement

To capitalise on the credit accumulation arrangements and to provide a common focus for the recording of achievement, NCVQ has also introduced the National Record of Vocational Achievement.[3] Since it was first used in September 1988, nearly a million copies have been issued, mainly in government funded programmes such as the Youth Training Scheme and Employment Training, but also in a number of colleges of further education and training centres.

The revised version which was introduced in 1990 includes a:

PERSONAL RECORD, which is the first section, available to hold a summary of school records of achievement, educational qualifications, CV and other information the holder of the record may wish to store,

ACTION PLAN which provides the targets for the current education or training programme. This would include details of the units of competence to be attempted in the case of NVQs,

ASSESSMENT RECORD which contains full details of units, elements and performance criteria of the learning programme and recorded assessments against these objectives, completed by the local assessor,

UNIT CREDITS; this section is to hold the certificates received from awarding bodies which show the units which have been achieved in the current programme and previously,

QUALIFICATIONS; the final section holds qualification certificates, which will increasingly be NVQs as the NVQ framework is established.

The National Record reflects the model presented in this book; all the above sections relate to the stages of the education and training process.

The National Record can be continued from one programme to the next, from one qualification to the next, and in fact provides a life long record of achievement. It should prove a particularly useful vehicle for encouraging the addition of units, possibly of a more specialized nature, or simply to update competence. Keeping abreast of new skills and techniques will be a growing requirement of employment.

NVQ Framework

To realize the full benefits of the National Record and credit accumulation and transfer system, one needs the comprehensive framework of NVQs, with each NVQ sub-divided into its units which are offered for independent assessment. In addition, we need to rationalize the NVQ framework so that those competences which are common to different NVQs, are expressed in the same way in common units.

An analysis of the functions within employment indicates that there is considerable overlap in what is performed in different jobs and different occupations. As units are based upon employment functions rather than the specific requirements of occupations or jobs, they can be stated independently of a job or occupation. As the NVQ framework develops, it is important to ensure that negotiations take place between the different industry and professional bodies responsible for setting standards, to achieve common units for the common functions. With such common units, credit transfer between qualifications and occupations will be automatic. This principle has already been established in the national system of credit accumulation and transfer.

Another indication of the scope for rationalization comes from experience of the Scottish Action Plan.[4] When non-advanced further education in Scotland was modularized, it reduced the provision from about 10,000 separate course-hours to 4000 course-hours, simply by restating that which was common in different programmes in the common modules.

Towards One National Record

Although the National Record of Vocational Achievement is less than two years old the concept has achieved wide acceptance. During the 1980s there has also been a growing interest in records of achievement in schools and widescale piloting and evaluation of different models. The school records have been largely concerned with capturing those achievements and experiences which fall outside formal qualifications. Such records also have an important role in formative assessment to facilitate learning. The Technical and Vocational Educational Initiative (TVEI) has also promoted records of achievement. The need to record National Curriculum attainments is a need identified for the future. The recent proposals put forward by the National Curriculum Council to incorporate the assessment and recording of core skills in A/AS levels, and more generally in post-16 education and training, includes the proposal for a record of achievement for this purpose.

Not surprisingly, given all these related requirements for records of achievement, there have been calls from many quarters for the introduction of a single national record, issued in schools and continuing into higher education and vocational and professional training. An extended version of the National Record of Vocational Achievement could fulfil this role. The non-formal and formative recording which is valued, particularly in schools, but also in other programmes could be accommodated in the one part, while more formal recording and certification associated with the National Curriculum, NVQs and other qualifications could be recorded in another. Action planning, which is likely to be more common in schools as well as in vocational training, and continuous assessment would also form part of the common record. The introduction of such a National Record would need to be managed by a consortium which included NCVQ, the National Curriculum Council and the Schools Education and Assessment Council.

A single record would do much to link education and training which have been divided for too long to the detriment of both. Almost all young people need to make the transition from the general or academic education system to vocational and professional training, whether after GCSE, A/AS levels or a degree. The form, structure and content of the two systems has not helped this transition in the past, nor has the low status accorded to training in comparison to education. Now there is an opportunity to break down this division. There are many encouraging signs of which moves towards a single record of achievement is one.[5]

Summary

Credit accumulation, and the associated unit structure of qualifications, greatly facilitates access to qualifications and flexibility in education and training. While some of the benefits can be realized within a single qualification, or those of one awarding body, there are significant additional benefits through the rationalization of qualifications within a national system. This allows credit transfer between the qualifications of different bodies and different occupations, professions and sectors. The NVQ framework opens up this possibility. A national record is the natural vehicle to co-ordinate credits within the system. The next step is establishing common outcomes to general education and vocational training, with credit transfer arrangements between the systems, through a common record of achievement.

10 The National Curriculum

The National Curriculum, which is now being phased into schools as part of the Education Reform Act of 1988, shares many features with the NVQ model. It represents a radical shift in school education towards the specification of outcomes. Just as vocational training will in future be targeted upon 'statements of competence', school education from five to 16 years will be targeted upon 'statements of attainment'.

The National Curriculum consists of the ten foundation subjects listed below. The first three, English, Mathematics and Science, are described as core subjects.

English
Mathematics
Science
Technology
History
Geography
Art
Music
Physical Education
A Modern Foreign Language (for children of secondary school age only)

(In Wales, Welsh will be a core subject in Welsh speaking schools and a foundation subject in other schools.)

The structure of the National Curriculum may be summarized as follows:

Each subject is sub-divided into a number of attainment targets representing different areas of the subject.

(e.g. in English there five attainment targets — speaking and listening, reading, writing, spelling and handwriting/presentation.

Within each attainment target, there may be up to 10 levels of attainment specified in the form of statements of attainment.

The structure can thus be represented as in insert 22:

INSERT 22: STRUCTURE OF THE NATIONAL CURRICULUM

SUBJECT

Profile Component 1	Profile Component 2	. . . .	Profile Component 3	. . . .
Attainment Target 1	Attainment Target 2	Attainment Target 3	Attainment Target 4	Attainment Target 5
St.Att 1	St.Att 1	St.Att 1	St.Att 1	St.Att 1
St.Att 2	St.Att 2	St.Att 2	St.Att 2	St.Att 2
St.Att 3	St.Att 3	St.Att 3	St.Att 3	St.Att 3
St.Att 4	St.Att 4	St.Att 4	St.Att 4	St.Att 4
St.Att 5	St.Att 5	St.Att 5	St.Att 5	St.Att 5
St.Att 6	St.Att 6	St.Att 6	St.Att 6	St.Att 6
St.Att 7	St.Att 7	St.Att 7	St.Att 7	St.Att 7
St.Att 8	St.Att 8	St.Att 8	St.Att 8	St.Att 8
St.Att 9	St.Att 9	St.Att 9	St.Att 9	St.Att 9
St.Att 10	St.Att 10	St.Att 10	St.Att 10	St.Att 10

(St.Att is short for 'Statement of Attainment')

(This is a simplified schematic representation, the number of Profile Components and Attainment Targets varies between subjects and there can be more than one Statement of Attainment at any level within an Attainment Target)

The statements of attainment are the most detailed specification in the NC, comparable to the elements of competence in the NVQ model. Assessment takes place in relation to each statement of attainment, as it does for elements in NVQs. An example of a statement of attainment is shown in insert[23].

Key Stages

Key stages are defined in terms of the age of the majority of children in a teaching group and assessments must take place at or near the end of each key stage. The key stages are approximately:

INSERT 23: EXAMPLE FROM THE NATIONAL CURRICULUM

subject: ENGLISH
Profile Component: Reading

Attainment Target: The development of the ability to read, understand and respond to all types of writing, as well as the development of information retrieval strategies for the purposes of study.

Statement of Attainment (at Level 9): Select, retrieve, evaluate and combine information independently and with discrimination, from a comprehensive range of reference materials, making effective use of the information.

(Example: Make use of techniques such as skim-reading and organizational devices such as layout, illustration and placing of visual images and text; and the production of text in a number of media, drawing on these devices).

Key stage 1 (5–7 years, infant)
Key stage 2 (7–11 years, junior)
Key stage 3 (11–14 years, secondary)
Key stage 4 (14–16 years, secondary).

Assessment and Testing

As with NVQs, assessment within the National Curriculum will be criterion-referenced, based directly upon explicit statements of the outcomes of learning required. Thus both what is to be learnt and assessed will be set out clearly in advance, in both NVQs and National Curriculum.

Unlike NVQs, the National Curriculum does not add performance criteria to the statements of attainment. It relies instead on the development of standard assessment tasks (SATs). SATs will by example imply the standard which is required in respect of a statement of attainment. The Department of Education and Science (DES) say of SATs that they are 'external prescribed assessments which may incorporate a variety of assessment methods. They will complement teachers' own assessments' (DES, 1989). DES also says: 'Teachers' own assessments are an essential part of the system. They will be able to cover aspects of performance not readily testable by conventional means, and more generally will ensure a place in the assessments for rounded, qualitative judgements' (DES, 1989). The balance between collecting evidence on a continuous basis, and using externally prescribed tests (SATs) in making decisions about attainment remains to be seen.

The National Curriculum Task Group on Assessment and Testing states:[1]

> Promoting children's learning is a principal aim of schools. Assessment lies at the heart of this process. It can provide a framework in which educational objectives may be set, and pupils' progress charted and expressed. It can yield a basis for planning the next educational steps in response to children's needs. By facilitating dialogue between teachers, it can enhance professional skills and help the school as a whole to strengthen learning across the curriculum and throughout its age range.

As with NVQs, assessment is perceived as an integral part of the learning process. It is however interesting to note that in the NVQ model, assessment would not be described as 'providing the framework in which educational objectives may be set'. The educational (or learning) objectives are set independently of assessment in statements of competence. This conceptual separation of statements of attainment and the assessment of such statements does not seem to have been made in the above report. The attainment targets and statements of attainment are not just an assessment framework, they are also a curriculum framework. The report does go on to say however:

> The assessment process itself should not determine what is taught and learned. It should be the servant, not the master, of the curriculum. Yet it should not simply be a bolt-on addition at the end. Rather, it should be an integral part of the educational process, continually providing both 'feedback' and 'feedforward'.

Assessment would be seen to serve precisely the same role in NVQs in addition to confirming achievement for certification.

Standard Assessment Tests (SATs) will be drawn up under direction of Schools Examination and Assessment Council (SEAC). For key stage 1, it will be unobtrusive and consist of a bank of tests from which the most appropriate may be selected. For 7 year olds, and largely for 11 year olds, the tests will take the form of topics for children to work on during which they will have to demonstrate a variety of achievements which teachers can observe and mark. There will be a range of tasks with different subjects and contexts which can be matched to the child's background and interests. For ages 14 and 16, subject-related tests will predominate.

Learning

The National Curriculum, which, unlike NVQs, will be supported by statutory programmes of study and will be delivered in a prescribed context, namely schools, provides controls which cannot be applied to NVQs. This is why the additional specification of performance criteria and range statements are necessary requirements of NVQs.

Schools are free to choose how to organize and teach the curriculum within the framework of the statutory programmes of study, attainment targets and assessment arrangements. They are also free to decide what other subjects they wish to teach beyond these requirements.

To summarize, the National Curriculum is expected to:

1 Provide clear objectives on which to base schemes of work and to which cross-curricular teaching can be related.
2 Provide a framework for continuity.
3 Provide for both progression and differentiation. 10 step level shows clearly the next level of attainment for each individual pupil.
4 Specify essential studies to be undertaken by all — schools may choose to adopt other subjects in addition to these.
5 There is no prescription on particular teaching methods or textbooks as part of a programme of study. Therefore there is considerable freedom for teaching
6 Most requirements are based on existing good practice and as such will be familiar to teachers. This will be supported to a great extent by existing materials and books.

It is expected that the attainment targets and programmes of study will be most comprehensive for the core subjects, although there will still be plenty of scope for teachers. In other foundation subjects the extent of cover by the targets and programmes will vary. The level of detail expected and required to be taught will also vary according to subject and key stage. The attainment targets for subjects such as maths are, predictably, much more detailed than for subjects like music, art and PE.

Wider Implications

The National Curriculum will result naturally in continuous assessment, through SATs and by other means integrated with the learning process. It will reduce, if not completely replace, in time, examinations at the end of large blocks of learning. The relationship between the achievement at Key Stage 4 and GCSE has still to be fully resolved.

The National Curriculum will expose more clearly the different rates of progress of students. The achievement of an attainment target at one level assumes that students will go on to attempt the next. To delay doing so would mean holding up and wasting the time of the student. The National Curriculum will also result in more individual and small group project work, and less class teaching. Both these factors point to more individualized programmes to meet the different needs of individuals at a given time. As the reader will have noted, all these features will be common to NVQs as well as the National Curriculum, because they are a consequence of adopting an outcome-led model of learning.

It is interesting to speculate on the effect the National Curriculum will have, first on A/AS levels, and subsequently on higher education. It is difficult to imagine that students coming through the National Curriculum, having spent the whole of their educational life in a system where the targets of learning are clearly stated, achievement is recorded against such targets, and learning is individualized, will settle down in the traditional A level/HE regime we have today.

The introduction of the National Curriculum represents a radical change in school education. At present the degree of central prescription and the detail of the specification is causing a good deal of concern amongst teaching staff, which is not surprising given the scale of the change.

11   Core Skills: Linking Education and Training

The idea that there are basic skills in areas such as communication, numeracy, problem solving, which can be applied to a wide range of activities, is of course not new. Nor are attempts to develop them in young people as a basis for future learning and performance. The 'three Rs' (reading, writing and arithmetic) were one conceptualisation of a 'core' education at an earlier period. The new methods of formulating outcomes in statements of competence and attainments has raised the question whether core skills can be assessed in this way. If core skills were to be part of the requirement for NVQs and/or educational qualifications, their status would be enhanced and their development taken more seriously.

The essential feature of core skills is that they are common to many activities. An NCVQ report on the topic states:[1]

> The essential point about the these facets of competence, and that which is central to their inclusion in this report, is the extent to which the skills are common to behaviour in different areas and contexts. If skills are common and widely applicable, or some aspect of the skill is common, it is that common aspect that we are defining as 'core'. This is based upon the assumption that the acquisition of the core skill in some areas of competence and contexts offers the potential of generalization or transfer to other areas and contexts which employ the same skill. We are therefore seeking to identify those aspects of skill which are common and transferable to a wide range of performance.

Developments to enhance the concept of competence in NVQs, by the incorporation of 'generic' competences or core skills were being considered in 1989, when proposals from the Department of Education and then the CBI added a new dimension to the introduction of core skills. Their respective proposals are summarized in insert 24.

Reports from the NCC and NCVQ, generated considerable interest in the possibility of creating a common framework of core skills which could be

INSERT 24: RECENT PROPOSAL FOR CORE SKILLS

CBI PROPOSAL FOR COMMON LEARNING OUTCOMES

In October 1989, the CBI proposed that the development of core skills or 'common learning outcomes' should be part of all education and training programmes for young people, from the age of 14 years. This was part of the broader CBI strategy to promote and expand education and training which is summarized at Appendix 'B'. Core skills were seen as a way of making education in schools more relevant to work and life and of improving transfer and progression in vocational training. Moreover, through the accreditation of a set of core skills which were common to education and training, links between the two systems would be established. The CBI referred to the development of NVQ core units as a way of addressing this issue.

DES PROPOSALS FOR CORE SKILLS IN A/AS LEVELS

Similar suggestions were made by Mr Kenneth Baker, when Secretary of State for Education, in a speech in February, 1989.[2] This was acted upon by his successor, Mr John MacGregor, in November 1989, when he asked the National Curriculum Council (NCC) to propose a set of core skills that could be incorporated in A/AS level programmes, and in post-16 education more generally.

The NCC reported their proposal to the Secretary of State in March 1990.[3] NCVQ simultaneouly published a report which dealt more specifically with the technical requirements for a framework of core skills which would be common and transferable between A/As levels and NVQs.[1] As the two Councils had worked closely together before publication, there was agreement on the core skills proposed.

The primary core skills, those which were considered to have almost universal application, were identified as;

  problem solving
  communication
  personal skills

NCVQ preferred the term 'personal autonomy' for the latter, but it referred to the same theme. NCC considered:

  numeracy
  information technology
  modern language competence

of equal importance, but could not see how these skills could form an integral part of all A/AS levels. They nevertheless recommended that their development should be promoted in the post-16 curriculum.

Both reports referred to the need to record achievements in core skills in a common record, possibly an extended version of the National Record of Vocational Achievement.

incorporated into both A/AS levels and NVQs. The core skills must first be defined as outcomes, in the form of elements of competence or statements of attainment. Since these statements will be independent of any qualification or programme of learning, they may be delivered within any programme. Using the NVQ assessment model, which allows evidence from any source provided it meets the performance criteria, evidence of the achievement of a core skill could be drawn either from projects and assignments within an A or AS level programme, or during demonstrations of competence for an NVQ.

Core skills will normally be developed and assessed as an integral part of a subject, such as History or Physics, or an occupational activity, such as Business Administration or Engineering. Core skills are already developed to some extent in such education or training programmes, but in future they will be assessed separately, and when performance critera are met, credit will be given for their achievement. This will have the effect of enhancing their development and ensure a range of core skills (initially problem solving, communication and some personal skills), are covered in all programmes. Insert 25, taken from a second NCVQ report on core skills,[4] shows how they might be assessed in NVQs.

If the same core skills can be developed and assessed in A/AS levels and NVQs, it will not only enhance both forms of provision, but facilitate transfer between the two systems. The potential implications of such an initiative are considerable.

The CBI report 'Towards a Skills Revolution' referred to NVQs at level III as being an equivalent achievement to 2 'A' levels. This was necessary to support their recommendation to provide entitlement to learning and to set national targets for achievement, spanning both education and training. (See Appendix 'B'). However, as 'A' levels and NVQs have different objectives and structures, there is no objective basis for drawing such equivalence. They are simply what one would expect 18 or 19 year olds to have achieved, through either full-time education or training.

The plan now is to see if it is possible to incorporate into the A/AS level curriculum and NVQs at level III, the same minimum level of achievement in the primary core skills. If this can be achieved it will establish a degree of genuine equivalence between the two forms of provision.

A further objective is to open access to higher education via NVQs at level III. 'A' levels are, of course, the normal entry requirement to universities and polytechnics. Entry through vocational routes is limited, but the BTEC National qualification, which equates roughly to NVQ level III, is recognised for entry to higher education. The objective is to build upon this precedent. Access from NVQs may become easier and more natural if there is a considerable expansion in HE provision, which many now seek.[5] It is also assumed that in the future there will be greater variety in what is on offer in the HE sector and in the modes of delivery. These issues are considered in Chapter 16.

INSERT 25: THE CONCEPT OF CORE SKILLS IN NVQs

It is proposed that core skills are incorporated into the NVQ system in the same format as units of competence. They would thus attract unit credits within the national systems of credit accumulation and transfer.

The fundamental core skills, problem solving, communication and personal skills, will normally be developed as an integral part of occupational competence leading to an NVQ. This already occurs, but trainees will probably be unaware of the fact. The performance demonstrations which are part of the assessment required for units of competence (e.g. reception duties) will also provide evidence for core skill units (e.g. communication). One objective of the core skill initiative would be to identify those core skills which are naturally developed as part of occupational competence and alert trainees to their potential transferability.

When the core skills currently identified in an NVQ are at a level below that required for core credits, attempts can be made to enhance their development. In most cases it is assumed this would usefully broaden the NVQ statement of competence. If the requirement for core skills cannot be met by enhancement alone, which is likely in some occupations, then, exceptionally, opportunities would need to be created to develop them which might extend the current concept of competence in the occupation. This would be achieved by the addition of related employment functions to expand what is currently covered by the NVQ. It is considered important that such additional activities to develop core skills are perceived as relevant to the needs of employers and the employment opportunities of trainees.

It must however be emphasised that such enhancement or extension does not mean that core skill units will be 'taught' or acquired separately from occupational units. Evidence of the achievement of core skills would be derived from occupational performance, and credit for core skills would be awarded as a by-product of the performance required for an NVQ.

The conscious acquisition of core skills by individuals will enhance their occupational competence and normally have immediate benefits for performance in employment. Moreover, it will provide a stronger foundation for transfer and progression, and the potential to cope with future changes in technology and work practices.

An example of how a core skill could be expressed as an element of competence is shown below.

INSERT 26: AN EXAMPLE OF A CORE SKILL ELEMENT IN PERSONAL AUTONOMY

ELEMENT: Identify personal strengths and weaknesses and set targets for self development in a range of applications and contexts

PERFORMANCE CRITERIA:

— An appropriate and relevant domain or range of domains in which strengths and weaknesses are to be identified is chosen.
— an appropriate and relevant range of evaluation and decision making framework for the identification of strengths and weaknesses is identified and accessed.
— an appropriate and sufficient amount of relevant personal data is collected and made available.
— specific, valid and reliable personal data is accurately and honestly matched against significant criteria from the appropriate evaluation frame.
— realistic and justifiable assessments are made of specific strengths and weaknesses within the criteria specified by the chosen frame.
— strengths and weaknesses are assessed accurately within the limitation of the evaluation instrument(s) and are clearly prioritised for future action.
— strengths and weaknesses which do not meet realistic requirements in the appropriate domain are targeted for development plans.
— realistic and achievable targets are set for self development in areas which do not meet realistic requirements to agreed and realistic timescales.

RANGE OF VARIABLES to which the element applies:

— as a learner, in interpersonal relations with fellow students or colleagues
— as an employee or prospective employee
— intellectual, personal physical.

(from NCVQ R&D Report No. 6, Common Learning Outcomes: Core Skills in A/AS levels and NVQs, Jessup, 1990)

If a common core skill framework is established for use in A/AS levels and NVQs at levels I to III, there is no reason why its application should stop there. Core skills are inevitably being developed within the National Curriculum and it would be natural for some credit to be given for their attainment. These would very likely overlap with those in NVQs at levels I and II, and could establish a bridge between the National Curriculum and NVQs, helping young people make the transition from school to training and work.

At the university level those institutions participating in the HE enterprise scheme, to promote enterprise training in university degrees, have expressed interest in the NVQ core credits. The scheme has much in common with that of core skills in A/AS levels. Some enterprise programmes are, for example, promoting problem solving and communication skills. One can foresee the core skill framework designed for A/AS levels and NVQs at levels I to III being extended to provide options in higher education and NVQs at levels IV and V.

Credit Transfer

Credit transfer between academic qualifications and NVQs need not be limited to core skills. Already there is discussion between the Schools Examinations and Assessment Council (SEAC) and NCVQ on the scope for credit transfer in areas which are common to academic qualifications and NVQs, such as information technology, foreign languages and business studies. Credit transfer will operate most effectively when credit is awarded for units or modules.

To collect together credits from the various awarding bodies and forms of provision, a unified record of achievement will be required. This is already on the agenda as discussed earlier.

Towards a Coherent Education and Training Framework

If the various developments to link education and training proceed one might picture the education and training provision in the future within a coherent framework as illustrated in insert 27. All young people will pursue the National Curriculum. At 16 years, some will continue in school or colleges through the A/AS level route, while others will take NVQs. There is a growing belief that everyone in the 16–18 age group should be in programmes leading to qualifications, either through full-time education and training, or through structured learning in the workplace or through a combination of on and off-the-job learning. Irrespective of the route or place of learning, all young people will be expected to develop common core skills. This will help to align the systems and facilitate transfer between them.

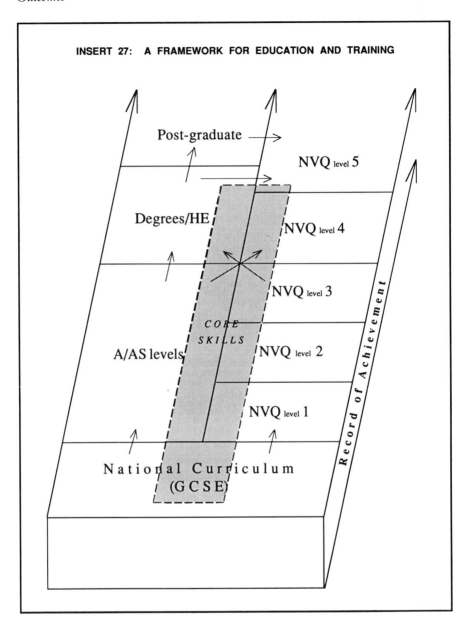

INSERT 27: A FRAMEWORK FOR EDUCATION AND TRAINING

Post-graduate

NVQ level 5

Degrees/HE

NVQ level 4

NVQ level 3

CORE SKILLS

A/AS levels

NVQ level 2

NVQ level 1

National Curriculum (GCSE)

Record of Achievement

An increasing number will be expected to participate in higher education and/or NVQs at level 4 and 5. There will also be frequent movement between general education and professional training, facilitated by credit transfer arrangements at all levels. The distinction between the largely separate systems which currently exist will become increasing blurred.

Part Two

The Model and its Implications

12   The Emerging Model

This chapter attempts to bring together the various concepts, processes and tools described in the previous chapters, and shows how they relate within a coherent model of education and training. The thesis put forward in this book is that if education or training is defined by its outcomes, it opens access to learning and assessment in ways which are not possible in traditional syllabus or programme based systems. Once learning is targeted on outcomes, the other features of the model follow as a natural consequence. Many of the problems we face in education and training could be solved by this model.

The model presented here is more than hypothetical in that parts of it are already being developed and introduced, if only on a limited scale so far. The model is also entirely consistent with current recommendations emanating from the CBI and TUC, and many aspects are being introduced to government programmes.[1] The essential features, in the order in which they occur in the learning cycle, are shown below.

Initial Assessment/Accreditation of Prior Learning

Before embarking upon any programme, learners and their advisers will want to assess the skills and knowledge they already possess to determine the appropriate starting point. This is especially important for adult learners, who will often have a variety of skills and knowledge upon which to build. Adults will also constitute an ever growing proportion of the participants in education and training in the future.

The normal practice will be to draw up a 'profile' of an individual's competence, including both formally recorded achievements such as educational and vocational qualifications and credits, and uncertificated competences acquired through experience at work or outside. Where practicable, evidence of competence from experience can be submitted for formal recognition through the process of the accreditation of prior learning (APL) considered in chapter 8.

Initial assessment and the accreditation of prior learning will be carried out in relation to the NVQ framework of education and training outcomes. This will provide a comprehensive spectrum of the competences required in employment in the form of elements, units and NVQs, the targets for learning, the requirements for assessment and the award of credit and qualifications.

The National Curriculum will provide the framework of educational outcomes. Although designed for five to 16 year olds, the statements of attainment are independent of age and the higher levels provide a framework which is suitable for most adults. It is recognized that only a minority of pupils will achieve National Curriculum level 10 (the highest) by the age of 16. The proposed core skill framework, equally relevant to NVQs and vocational education and training as A/AS levels and general education, will extend the range of competence which can be recognised.

The above frameworks should be in place in the early 1990s, and will cover the ground which is relevant to the achievements of the majority of people. In later chapters we speculate on the possibility of an entire education and training system being based upon outcomes, creating the possibility of an overall framework for general education and training.

The detail of the frameworks, all the statements of competence and attainment, will naturally be available on computer databases. Such a database already exists for NVQs. Individuals and their advisers can easily access the data through personal computers. Initial assessment and the accreditation of prior learning will be made in conjunction with the databases. Individuals will be able to develop profiles of their achievements to date, with the help of advisers as required. It will be possible to print out such profiles for inclusion in one's Record of Achievement.

Guidance

Following initial assessment, the next stage in the model is discovering what learning opportunities (normally in the form of outcomes, packaged as units, attainment targets and qualifications) would be an appropriate next step for the learner. In practice guidance would be provided at each stage and be available at the same time as initial assessment. The NVQ framework is designed to indicate potential routes of progression. Information on the relationship between occupations, qualifications and education and training will be far superior to anything available in the past. This will be the result of organizing structures, such as the NVQ framework and the use of electronic databases. The NVQ database, in addition to the functions already described, also provides a new tool for guidance. Users will be able to explore occupational areas and find out, in considerable detail if necessary, both the functions performed in any occupation and the requirements to become competent and qualified in an occupation.

Some individuals will enter the process with clear and realistic goals needing little guidance. Others will be less certain and wish to explore alternatives. Some users will be able to make their own decisions on what is appropriate based upon the information available with little or no help. Others may require considerable help. Career guidance will thus not follow a set procedure but will be tailored to individual needs.

Apart from guidance on careers and related education and training routes, guidance should also be available on education and training provision and consideration of suitable modes of learning. Information about the provision of learning opportunities will also be made more systematically available in future through computerised databases. Computerised systems such as Training Access Points (TAPs) and Educational Counselling and Credit Transfer Information Service (ECCTIS) already exist, although they are not widely used, and there are directories of open learning materials. These systems are not co-ordinated nor are they systematically linked to qualification systems or occupations or professions. The NVQ framework and database now provide an organizing structure to relate these different sources of information. At the time of writing, links between the NVQ database and TAPs and ECCTIS are being explored. In the future it should be possible to move from the identification of units and NVQs, directly through linked databases to the learning opportunities available to achieve them.

Information on the local provision at colleges, training centres and in companies could be entered locally in an extension to the NVQ database. Open learning and other NVQ support materials could be designed nationally and information could be made available on a nationally linked database.

Action Planning

Individual action plans have recently become accepted in vocational education and training, even if not widely or very effectively practised as yet. Action planning stems directly from individualized learning, which in turn follows naturally once an individual's initial profile of competence is taken into account. Action plans can be set out in different ways but they all incorporate targets for future learning which should be negotiated and agreed between the learner and the providers of learning opportunities.

In the model developed here it is assumed that the primary action plan targets will be the units of competence and NVQs, which have been identified at the previous stage. The targets could also be National Curriculum attainment targets or other qualifications, provided there was sufficient flexibility in the way they could be achieved. One can envisage action plans in the future, especially those of young people, often including a mixture of vocational and educational targets.

Action plans also provide scope for identifying and including targets which fall outside the formal qualification system. These will include specific company or organizational goals and personal goals.

Action plans should also contain the programme by which the targets will be achieved. This will include the mode of learning, location or context of learning and timescales. Action plans should be reviewed and revised during the course of the learning programme as necessary.

Completed action plans related to NVQs and vocational targets can be inserted in the National Record of Vocational Achievement, for which provision is already made. In the future one can foresee a single National Record which will incorporate action plans and achievements in both educational and vocational programmes.

Programmes of Learning

The form of the programme to be undertaken is set out in the individual action plan. As we have seen, to maximize participation, learning opportunities will be provided in a variety of forms, contexts and timescales.

The NVQ framework provides a structure within which to organize a national system of programmes and learning materials. There are proposals to design a national system of open learning and support materials targeted on NVQ units. These could have mass application, which would make it economical to produce them to a very high quality.

The individual will normally be expected to take greater responsibility for his or her own learning in the new model than under the old systems, although there should be guidance available throughout a programme to support those who need it. It is important, as learning will frequently take place in more than one location during a programme, that guidance supports the integration of learning from different sources.

Continuous Assessment

Continuous assessment will be normal practice within the model, although there will be exceptions where final examinations still prevail, for at least part of the assessment. It is most economical and natural to carry out assessment at a time when competences are practised and demonstrated. As we have seen there are also considerable technical advantages in making assessment decisions on an accumulation of evidence over time rather than on a single test.

Assessment will frequently require the accumulation of evidence from different locations and from different assessors, reflecting the different contexts of learning. This points to the need of systematic recording and the co-ordinated management of the process. The National Record of Vocational

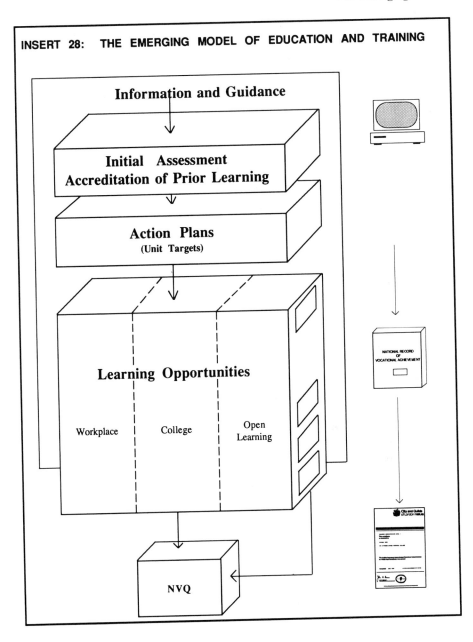

INSERT 28: THE EMERGING MODEL OF EDUCATION AND TRAINING

Information and Guidance

Initial Assessment
Accreditation of Prior Learning

Action Plans
(Unit Targets)

Learning Opportunities

Workplace   College   Open Learning

NVQ

Achievement incorporates the facility for recording assessments. The National Record is held by the individual in whose name it is issued and he or she must accept some responsibility for ensuring recording takes place and is co-ordinated. Continuous assessment will also be a feature of the National Curriculum with a procedure for recording the achievement of statements of attainment and the attainment targets.

Unit Credits

Along with continuous assessment goes credit accumulation (its advantages as described in chapter 9). We have seen that NVQs are made up of units which can be separately accredited. Unit credits are currently recorded in an individual's National Record and we look forward to the day when there is a single record which incorporates achievements in schools and beyond. Even now summaries of achievements in schools can be included in the first part of the National Record of Vocational Achievement and assist in initial assessment and action planning towards NVQs.

Completion of Action Plan

The final stage in the model is the completion of the action plan which in the vocational field may result in the award of an NVQ. The NVQ certificates awarded are also stored in the National Record to complete the learning cycle.

In the new model, learning is regarded as a continuing process and the end of one action plan will frequently be followed by the start of another, if not immediately, then some time later. The cycle will thus be repeated. The model envisages continuous learning.

Insert 28 illustrates the model and how it applies to NVQs.

13　Implications For Employers

The new model of education and training (or learning) assumes that companies and other employing organizations will become major providers of learning opportunities. There is already an increasing number of 'work experience placements' being provided for short periods for school pupils through a variety of national programmes and local initiatives. The new emphasis being placed on the systematic development and accreditation of core skills, first in A/AS levels and NVQs, plus other moves to bridge the gap between education and training, and school and work, can only reinforce this trend. Placements and sandwich years are common to various forms of higher education.

The Youth Training Scheme (YTS), and its successor Youth Training (YT), have established learning through structured work experience, on a very large scale. The Employment Training scheme (ET) has extended the practice to include adults. Many participants in YTS/YT and ET have the status of employees while training. The distinction between training for employment, and employment while training is becoming less clear, as is the distinction between work and learning.

The next step, conceptually not large but logistically huge, is to create an infrastructure and a culture within companies and other employing organizations, in which it becomes normal practice for employees at all levels, to continue learning and enhancing their competence. This, of course, already happens to varying degrees at varying levels within companies. But what is now being contemplated is a structured process of learning, going beyond the requirements of current jobs, in preparation for a more dynamic and demanding industrial environment.

If we briefly review some recent pronouncements by employers and government we can get a picture of the scale of the change required. The reference to a 'skills revolution' and a 'quantum leap forward' by the CBI would seem to be well founded:

all young people should be given an entitlement to structured training, work experience or education leading to NVQ level III or its
academic equivalent (ie 2 'A' levels and 5 GCSEs at A–C grades),

by 1995, all employees should take part in company-driven training
or developmental activities as the norm,

by 1995, at least half of the employed workforce should be aiming
for updated or new qualifications within the NVQ framework, preferably in the context of individual action plans and with the support
from employers,

by the year 2000, 50 percent of the employed workforce should be
qualified to NVQ level III or its academic equivalent as a minimum

(Targets set in Towards a Skills Revolution, CBI, November, 1989 and
subsequently endorsed by the Secretary of State for Employment, Norman
Fowler, see Appendix 'B').

It will be appreciated that the CBI, TUC and government (and other
political parties) are not simply talking about improving the initial education
and training of new entrants to the workforce, although this is part of the
plan. For one reason, we cannot afford to wait a generation or so for the
new entrants gradually to raise the average level of the competence of the
workforce. As many have pointed out, 80 percent of the current workforce
will still be in employment in the year 2000. For another, the new entrants to
the workforce will also need continuing training to update and improve their
skills, and to adapt to changing work requirements.

It is recognized that the upgrading of the competence of the workforce
cannot be achieved by attendance on external courses. The money and time
which employers and the government would need to allocate to an external
programme of the scale required could not be contemplated. Nor would it be
possible to build a few thousand extra colleges overnight and staff them even
if the billions were made available. Employees would not respond to such an
initiative anyway. The last thing many wish to do is to return to any place
that reminds them of school. The workplace must become the primary
location of learning, although support from a wide variety of external
agencies will be needed.

Nevertheless, if we use the workplace as the primary location for continuing learning, that learning cannot be limited simply to the short term
needs of companies. To realize the objectives sought by the government, the
CBI, the TUC and all national agencies, we must ensure that training is
targeted on national standards. By doing so employers will also ensure
that their workforce is more flexible and adaptable, and better prepared to
cope with changes in technology and work practices.

A practical advantage of basing training on national standards is that it becomes economical to provide centrally, a range of support mechanisms and materials. The further education service can be geared up to support companies and a national infrastructure of databases, guidance services and learning materials can be provided. To create the conditions within companies and organisations in which training could take place on the scale envisaged, or even approach it, will require initiatives of the kind indicated below:

Training or the development of human resources will need to be written into the corporate plans of every company and time and money will need to be devoted to it.

Managers and supervisors will need to have the development of their staff written clearly into their job descriptions and they will themselves require training to become trainers (or more specifically the planners and facilitators of learning).

Managers and supervisors will also need to become assessors, of which the major component will be an awareness of the national standards required by employees in their occupations in addition to the standards applied to their immediate jobs.

Jobs will need to be analysed to see what learning opportunities they provide. The experience of employees will need to be extended through job rotation and job enlargement. Placements of employees in other companies and exchanges of employees between companies may further extend learning opportunities.

In addition to learning directly through work, experience will normally need to be supplemented by inputs of training at colleges, company training centres, open learning, computer assisted learning or by other means.

Companies will need to institute a system for planning, record keeping, monitoring progress and so on. Fortunately this can be largely computerized. Companies would all be registered as training centres and approved as assessment centres for the award of credits and qualifications.

Consortia arrangements will need to be established between companies and local providers of education and training. This is clearly most important for small employers, but applies to all. Training Enterprise Councils (TECs) have been set up to stimulate the creation of such arrangements in their locality. The provision of learning will be a multi-agency activity; co-ordination will be all important.

In addition, there will be a need for the following to support the learning arrangements, although they will not necessarily be supplied by companies:

Excellent information sources, freely accessible by all participants, on the framework of standards, qualifications, units and related learning opportunities of all kinds. (These will of course be on linked computer databases.)

Guidance services providing impartial advice to learners, to interpret and supplement the information available. This will be associated with initial assessment and the accreditation of prior learning services leading to individual action planning. These services are probably best provided on behalf of a local consortium in order to extend access to a range of assessment facilities, to make best use of the expertise required for these functions and to preserve a professional detachment from the vested interests of companies and providers.

The steps outlined above to provide a learning culture within companies will only come about through a high degree of commitment by senior management to raise standards of performance and to plan beyond their immediate needs. It will also require a high degree of commitment by government to support such changes, not necessarily with large amounts of money, but by ensuring that there are incentives for companies and individuals to invest in training. In addition, the education and training services, which are largely funded publicly, must be geared up to support companies move in the direction indicated.

A Change of Culture

To achieve the learning society within industry we shall need a cultural shift, not only in the way employers view training, but also in the attitudes of employees. To achieve this, training and qualifications have got to be valued by individuals. They must have meaning in terms of an employee's own aspirations and expectations.[1]

In summary, the targets set by the CBI and TUC, and generally supported by government, call for a massive expansion of training within companies on a scale never before envisaged. The model proposed here provides a potential means of achieving this.

14   Implications for Further Education

The move towards the outcome-based model as exemplified by the introduction of NVQs will have profound effects on the institutions providing vocational education and training. Some of these effects will also be felt
in schools through the introduction of the National Curriculum and related
initiatives.

Learning as the Central Process

One vital change necessary is to recognise that the key process on which to
concentrate is not the teaching or training by the providers, but that of
learning by the students or trainees, the clients in the system. The role of
teachers and trainers is to facilitate learning, they cannot control the process.
Learning is primarily the responsibility of the learner, particularly when the
learner is a mature adult as most people pursuing NVQs will be. Learners
should be encouraged to take this responsibility.

Learning is not limited to the courses, programmes and packages devised
by educators and trainers, but can take many forms and occur in many
places. We can learn much through experience and reflection upon that
experience.

Individualized Learning

NVQs point towards individualized learning programmes, although this
ideal will not always be realized. If we accept that people enter a new phase
of learning with different baselines of educational attainment and competence, what they will need to learn to reach the same target will be
different. Again if in the future we are dealing with a more diverse group of
clients, many with considerable prior experience, the truth of this will be
even more evident. Nor will learners necessarily want to pursue the same

targets. Some will wish only to achieve a particular set of units. Others may wish to pursue particular options within an NVQ.

Not only will the content covered vary between learners, but also the time they have available to acquire new skills, the opportunities to learn through work or otherwise and their preferred modes of learning.

For all of these reasons what most learners will want is an individual action plan, which will set out both the units to be covered and the way (location and mode of learning) in which the competences will be acquired.

Information, Guidance and Counselling

As we have seen from the model, individuals will need considerable help and encouragement to participate in the initial assessment and accreditation of their prior learning if they are to take advantage of the opportunities available. Staff in colleges and training centres will need to acquire new skills themselves in assessment and guidance. The information and guidance must be objective and not relate solely to what their college or centre can provide.

Assessment

Even if centres do not take on the full guidance and counselling role, their staff will need to acquire expertise in the new forms of assessment which are a key feature at all stages in the delivery of NVQs. This is not to suggest that the new approach to assessment is unduly complicated. For those with no previous experience of assessment and examining it will probably seem quite straightforward. The main problems will lie with those who are set in the traditional model of assessment of formal tests and examinations.

Central to assessment in NVQs is a full appreciation of the statement of competence on which assessment is based, particularly the elements of competence, performance criteria and range statements. If these are understood in detail the evidence requirements will follow naturally. All that will often be necessary is to observe some basic guidelines about the sufficiency of the evidence.

It seems reasonable to expect teachers and trainers, particularly if they are full-time professionals, to acquire a full appreciation of the statements of competence in their subject area. This, after all, will be the content of their subjects or occupations and will also determine the learning opportunities they create and the instruction they provide. But both in their 'teaching' and in the assessment for NVQs they will have to think afresh what is required rather than relying on repeating standard scripts and materials. There will of course be new support materials developed for trainers, and also the learners, targeted directly on NVQ statements of competence.

Above all, we must not persist in viewing assessment as we have, often quite rightly in the past, as an unwanted addition to the process of learning which distorts the aims of the curriculum. In the new model assessment is a natural and integral part of the learning process.

Provision of Learning Opportunities

The NVQ model requires learning programmes tailored to meet the specific needs of individuals. The ideal model will not always be realised but it is important to appreciate that this would be the most efficient from the viewpoint of the learner. In practice there will be a trade-off between the economies of offering some standard set of instructional inputs, for some parts of a programme for groups of trainees, and tailoring each part of the programme for an individual's needs.

The practising of skills and the performances required to achieve competence has by its nature tended to be more individualised than instruction in the knowledge and theory. In training workshops trainees often work on their own projects and even when trainees are doing the same thing, it is quite common, and acceptable, for them to work at different speeds. Learning within individualised programmes can be seen as an extension of such practices.

Not only will learners be carrying out their own projects and assignments at their own pace, but they will frequently be working through support materials which complement the practice. These could be in written form, or on video or computer based. The teacher's or trainer's role would be to support, encourage, and guide such learning as required, and to observe and assess.

Ideally it should normally be the learner, when feeling competent in an aspect of the programme, who asks to be assessed. Such assessment may entail checking a product or outcome of an assignment, although the teacher or trainer would frequently have additional evidence from continuous observation which would contribute to the assessment decision. The new-style trainer would naturally provide feedback on assessments and guidance on any aspects of performance which needed further attention. Assessments would be recorded and any adjustments to the action plan would be discussed.

Projects can also be based upon group activity where the nature of the competence and circumstances are appropriate. Learners can help and motivate each other within or outside group learning. This is a well recognized practice in the training of senior managers and professionals, and in for example, Montessori schools for pre-school children, but is often forgotten in between.

This model of learning requires a degree of maturity on the part of the learner. If learners are treated as responsible people and responsible for their own learning they are more likely to respond accordingly. Of course, if individuals have lost, or never acquired, the habit of structured learning they will need more support and encouragement and it should be made available. It will be a style of learning which people will increasingly come to expect from a young age. There is plenty of evidence from primary schools, and even pre-primary schools, that very young children can pursue individualised learning programmes as members of a group, so it should not be too much to ask of young people and adults taking NVQs. Where there are problems it is perhaps a comment on the education process individuals have experienced since primary school.

This approach, which places more responsibility for learning on the learner, will, it is hoped, carry over to continuing learning beyond the programme. In fact one does not have to think in terms of programmes but simply continuing learning, although action plans, accumulating units and qualifications provide direction, structure and a sense of achievement and progress.

Learning Resource Centres

The above model, designed on the needs of the learner, may create considerable upheaval for institutions currently providing courses and programmes. The most radical change will be from the delivery of courses, with programmed start dates, scheduled classes, and fixed termination dates, often fitting in with the seasons of an academic year, for a given number of students, to individualised programmes, starting and ending at different times. In addition, colleges and training centres can expect to expand their client population to include far more adult employees and women returning to training and work, who will require a variety of specialized offerings.

The programmes of most future learners will take place partly or mainly in the workplace. Some of these programmes will be managed from a college or training institution, in which case tutors or trainers will need to liaise with the workplace providers to plan the programme. Sometimes the situation will be reversed with the company assuming responsibility for the management of the programme and negotiating with the college to supply part of the learning input required.

If these changes are to succeed some adaptation or expansion of the role of colleges and training centres will be called for. It might be helpful if those who managed colleges and training centres thought of their institutions as learning resource centres, able to provide a variety of services to clients.

Clients, who may be either individuals or bodies such as companies, local authorities or TECs, will need access to the following services:

— information and advice on competences required for occupations and opportunities for progression;
— information and advice on the provision of learning opportunities;
— initial assessment and the accreditation of prior learning;
— individual action planning;
— management for the implementation of action plans;
— learning opportunities for those parts of the plans which the centre has contracted to provide;
— guidance, support and tuition throughout the learning programmes;
— libraries of open learning and support materials, plus access to national networks of such materials;
— computer terminals and video facilities to access learning materials in these media;
— continuous assessment for those trainees undergoing learning programmes;
— recording and administration in respect of certification.

There should be open access to the assessment and guidance services whether an individual is taking advantage of the learning opportunities offered by the centre or not.

In addition, learning resource centres should normally become centres of expertise for:

— the development of learning materials;
— the development of assessment instruments.

And they should also offer the following external services to the local community:

— guidance to companies on providing in-house learning opportunities;
— in-company guidance and tutoring to individuals and groups;
— in-company assessment of employees;
— in-company training of supervisors and managers in supporting the learning of their staff;
— in-company training in assessment;
— extending the use of the centres' open learning materials and related facilities to support in-company training.

An example of a further education college that is changing in order to adopt the new model of education and training is Wirral Metropolitan College. The college's central aim is now 'personal achievement'. Its mission statement is shown in insert 29.

INSERT 29: THE WIRRAL COLLEGE MISSION STATEMENT

Personal achievement is the core of the college's mission statement. The document states:

1 Personal achievement is every individual's right, and the College should organize itself behind this right.
2 The establishment of personal achievement is a powerful aid to learning and motivation; it should be seen primarily in these terms, within a framework of standards.
3 The physical, mental and psychological involvement of learners with their own development and achievement, and that of their peers, should be adopted as an organizing principle for the College;
4 Personal achievement should constitute the core mission of the College. To encourage the College to be self-critical about its ability and preparedness to support personal growth, positive appraisal measures should be introduced and developed for learning, teaching and learner support.

The publication later says;

'Achievement-led institutional development facilitates the delivery of NVQs by distinguishing assessment and certification from courses and teaching.'

The colleges priorities for the next 12 months were:

1 the establishment of a collegiate admissions service with standard features in respect of information, diagnostic assessment, advice and record raising;
2 the introduction of NROVA for all full-time and as many part-time students as possible, and incorporating a formative record-system for TVEI purposes;
3 the establishment of individual learning workshops for an educational core comprising communications, mathematics, IT and science and technology;
4 the identification of core requirements and achievements in vocational courses;
5 the organization of courses into vocational, generic/core, and integrating components;
6 the establishment of college centres for study, support and assessment.

(Reproduced from 'An achievement-led college', Jenny Shackleton, in Competency Based Education and Training. Ed. John W. Burke, Falmer Press, 1989)

The Wirral Metropolitan College has made much progress towards realizing its objectives since the above statements were drafted two years ago.

Attitudinal Change

As significant as the institutional changes are the changes in attitude by staff in colleges if the new model of learning is to be fully successful. The introduction of NVQs changes the traditional role of the teacher/lecturer as we have seen in previous chapters. They will need considerable support as

---

INSERT 30: ANXIETIES WITH NEW PRACTICES

from 'Attitudinal change in FE in response to the introduction of NVQs', in Competency Based Education and Training, Ed. John W. Burke, Falmer Press, 1989

Some lecturers who had already started teaching NVQs experienced a range of concerns. The change from lecturing to a whole class, to a more student-centred approach, caused practical difficulties and was more demanding. One said she felt she might lose the esteem of her colleagues; she might be perceived as taking the easy way out. And there were ethical worries. Was she doing a good job? Were her students benefiting? Did her colleagues appreciate her difficulties:

> I think they [fellow lecturers] need a change of attitude all round really. From the management point of view I think we need classes to be smaller because when you're going round a class of fifteen all doing different things it is exhausting, far harder than standing up and teaching them all the same thing at the same time. And yet there tends to be an attitude, 'well you're not really teaching them', because, say I've got seven of them [business students] I'll give a booklet we've done for teach yourself subjects; one, two, three and four would be doing something else another four would be doing something else and they — well you're not really teaching them are you? They're teaching themselves. And from some of the students you get that as well, 'You haven't taught that, Miss. It's really from the book'.

> ... And this may have some sort of ethical, moral concerns on both the part of the teachers who is conscientious and wonders 'Am I giving my best?' And also the students who might think, 'Oh am I getting a thin deal?'.

well as staff development to adapt to their new role. In many respects it will be more demanding, but it should also be more rewarding. Lecturers will need to be more than subject specialists and think more about the process of learning. Identifying learning difficulties through assessment, which will be integral to the learning process, and how such difficulties might be overcome will be part of the role.

The introduction of the new model will also require a review of the way in which education and training is financed. Some new practices are being discouraged because they do not attract government subsidies, which are largely based on the assumption that education is provided to groups in classes on specified courses. A related issue is the reward systems, both real and perceived, which operate within colleges. Unless lecturers are positively encouraged to provide flexible learning routes and are judged on *what* their students learn, rather than *how*, it is unlikely that the new model will take root in colleges. One method by which the new Training Enterprise Councils will be evaluated is on the outcomes achieved by trainees, as measured by NVQs and other qualifications. This is more in accord with the model.

There is now growing experience from colleges on the early introduction of NVQs.[1] There are a wide range of initiatives and developments, supported by the Training Agency, the Department of Education, the Further Education Unit (FEU) and NCVQ, to promote and evaluate the introduction of NVQs. Insert 31 presents some observations from an evaluation of a major programme co-ordinated by FEU.

INSERT 31: IMPLEMENTATION IN COLLEGES

extracts from 'Implementation in colleges of FE' by Ian Haffende and Alan Brown, in Competency Based Education and Training, ed. John W Burke, Falmer Press, 1989

When considering the response of staff throughout a college to the implications of NVQs for curriculum development, it was clear that two factors were particularly significant in raising general awareness. Firstly, if the college was actively involved in national or regional development work. Involvement in pilot projects or other development work heightened awareness elsewhere in the college, although the extent to which opportunity was built upon depended largely upon the second factor; whether there was a clear institutional lead in making such connections.

The effect of the NVQs on course organization was seen as profound. There was a recognition among many of the more aware tutors that college wide responses to reorganizing the curriculum would be required. For example, the need to secure greater involvement and in-

---

tegration with industry, which in turn would require industry liaison time. Similarly, with the increasing modularization of courses, staff time on the design, development, production and assessment of materials would need to be allocated. The role of course teams was seen to be likely to become more significant in putting such programmes together, providing support and guidance in the lecturer's changing role, including increasing student counselling responsibilities. Indeed, the variety of skills required might mean that rather than individual lecturers being expected to be able to undertake all of these duties, there might be increasing specialization. In such circumstances, course teams would become even more vital.

Additionally, it was pointed out that colleges will need to look carefully at the implications of continuous assessment replacing end of year examinations, standardized courses across departments and the need to reduce staff-student ratios to accommodate changes in style and method of delivery. The structure of courses will then require radical reassessment, not least because for financial reasons pressure will be on to increase rather than reduce staff-student ratios. To some extent it may be possible to reconcile the competing pressures by having fewer formal classes with teachers operating in a didactic mode. Greater independent learning, coupled with mixing of a number of groups/individuals working in the same room with a tutor acting as a common resource may help offset the cases where a tutor has to work with very small groups or even individuals (although in such circumstances one could question the efficacy of staff-student ratios as a meaningful indicator of efficiency or performance).

The delivery of courses was seen as an area which will be particularly affected by the introduction of NVQs. For example, college staff expect that formal teaching will decline with more practical work and open and individualized learning replacing it. They see their role changing with more administration and assessment together with responsibility for designing and facilitating learning. New skills will be needed to achieve this, including the ability to design and write learning programmes which enable assessment of competence to a range of specified standards.

Of all the changes National Vocational Qualifications are likely to bring about, it is their affect on assessment that is causing greatest concern. Where some college staff feared the marginalization of college involvement altogether as a result of increased workbased assessment, others clearly saw a new role for them in moderation and standards monitoring.

NVQs are being introduced in colleges of further and higher education at a time when they are having to adjust to the changes imposed by the 1988 Education Reform Act. Colleges are expected to become more entrepreneurial in marketing their services to industry and more responsive to individual and employer needs. Although NVQs are seen by some colleges as an additional burden with which to cope, others recognise that they provide a means of offering the more flexible and relevant provision which is needed. NVQs can be regarded as part of the solution rather than another problem.

15   Implications for General Education

The changes we can anticipate in school education will be similar in direction to those described for vocational education and training, but less pronounced. School is context, age and institution bound, unlike adult education and training, and this imposes certain constraints. With the introduction of the National Curriculum for five to 16 year-olds we can expect significant changes in the style of learning. As argued earlier, the specification of learning outcomes has logical consequences.

The form of the attainment targets and statements of attainment in the National Curriculum will promote more active learning (doing things). Attainment targets start with a verb (retrieve, select, identify, devise etc.) which implies a mode of activity which effects both assessment and learning. It is interesting to note that attainment targets are accompanied by 'standard assessment tasks' (SATs) which further clarify what is expected in delivering the curriculum and provide a means of assessment. The word 'task' clearly points to an active, task-oriented, form of learning. The term was chosen in preference to 'test' to encourage a wider range of approaches to assessment in schools. The National Curriculum Task Group on Assessment and Testing stated:[1]

> Standard assessments need not only be in written form. Indeed, the wide variety of possibilities can be explored by analysing any one task in terms of three aspects or modes, which can be defined as follows:
>
> — the presentation mode — the method of delivery of the questions (oral, written, pictorial, video, computer, practical demonstration);
> — the operation mode — the expected method of working (mental only, written, practical, oral);
> — the response mode — pupils may answer in various ways (eg choosing one option in a multiple-choice question, writing a short prescribed response, open ended writing, oral, practical procedure observed, practical outcome or product, computer input).

> The art of constructing good assessment tasks is to exploit a wide range (far wider than those normally envisaged for tests) of modes of presentation, operation and response, and their numerous combinations, in order to widen the range of pupils' abilities that they reflect and so enhance educational validity.' (Para 47 and 48).

Task or project based learning also points towards more individualized learning and small group activity. Under the National Curriculum, the greater recognition of individual differences, both in terms of the amount of support and tuition required and the speed of learning, will accentuate this trend.

All this implies greater demands on teachers.[2] They will need to think more about different approaches to learning, carry out more diagnosis of learning difficulties and provide less standard inputs to the whole group. Given the average size of classes, compromises will need to be made, but the teacher does not need to be seen as the only resource in the classroom. Learning can be supported by a variety of learning materials to which the students can have direct access. Moreover, students can support each other. The students who progress more quickly can provide help to others. It is well recognized that one often only really finds out whether one understands something when trying to explain it to someone else. Teaching is a form of learning.

The modes of assessment in the National Curriculum should lead to less competition and more mutual support than traditional examinations. This could be positively fostered. It would be worth considering building into the curriculum a further attainment target concerned with facilitating the learning of other students. Thus students would be judged not only on their individual performance in a subject but also to the extent they helped others improve their performance. Apart from the benefits this could bring to raising the average levels of performance in schools, the long term contribution to the learning society we wish to create in companies and elsewhere could be immense. The social benefits in the attitudes this would foster will also be evident to the reader.

A/AS Qualifications

There is a widespread view that with all the reforms taking place in education and training, that post-16 education in schools, notably the A/AS levels, cannot remain unchanged. The Higginson Report[2] on A/AS levels, which pre-dated much of the thinking contained in this book, considered A/AS levels too narrow and specialised for today's needs and recommended a broader provision consisting of five subjects. But this was not acted upon by government. The requirements for A/AS level qualifications have been largely determined by the function they serve as entry qualifications to higher education. There is a fear that any change in A/AS levels may be detrimental to their 'academic rigour', although this concept is not very clearly defined.

INSERT 32: LIFE WITHOUT TEACHER IN THE SIXTH FORM

extracts from The Independent on Sunday, Judith Judd, 22 July, 1990
A new scheme in Northumberland helps students to help themselves

'organizing their own time is probably the most difficult skill sixth formers have to learn.' Yet this ability is vital if students are to survive when they leave school for higher education, where they receive far less guidance. A new scheme in Northumberland's sixth forms aims to provide pupils with the help they need. This self-study programme ensures that they spend less time with their teachers and more working on previously prepared material, on their own or in small groups.

In Northumberland the programme has another purpose. Because it involves less teaching time than conventional sixth-form work, it is seen by the council as a way of offering a broad range of subjects in small sixth forms in widely dispersed secondary schools. Ultimately, the authority expects to be able to offer A-levels in schools where there is no specialist teacher in the subject. Students would work through self-study materials, helped by a visiting specialist and a teacher from within the school itself.

Chris Boothroyd, education manager for Northumberland's director of education ... 'It doesn't follow that children are absorbing something just because a teacher is standing in front of a class teaching them. Employers and higher education institutions don't want that sort of passive learning which goes on when a teacher is telling a class facts. Students have taken part in this kind of process ever since Socrates. We have become more aware of it recently through the Open University, open learning and GCSE course work, but good schools have always encouraged pupils to work independently'.

Facilities which students can use on their own include videos, computer programs and audios tapes as well as conventional written materials. It is left to teachers to judge how often a tutorial is needed. Usually, there is at least one a fortnight. In all subjects, students are encouraged to assess their own work and to help one another ...

'I should like to see this type of learning spread like a benevolent virus through the system,' [says Michael Duffy, head of King Edward VI School]. 'You have to get away from the old idea that, unless staff are holding forth, they are not teaching. Teachers need to shut up and sit back'.

Some changes are nevertheless being pursued. The recent initiative by the Secretary of State for Education, to ensure that core skills are developed in all A/AS level provisions, as well as NVQs, is likely to have significant implications (see chapter 11). There are also a variety of experimental schemes, spurred on by the Technical and Vocational Educational Initiative (TVEI), which are offering modular 'A' levels and encouraging continuous assessment and records of achievement. Related to the core skill initiative, there are proposals to explore the scope for credit transfer between A/AS levels and NVQs, where the former are covering vocationally relevant subjects (eg business studies, information technology, foreign languages).

These changes, together with the expectations of young people emerging from the National Curriculum with the NVQ model gaining ground alongside, are likely to create pressure towards the adoption of an outcome model for A/AS qualifications. It should also be noted that 41 per cent of A/AS level qualifications are taken in FE colleges and not schools. Here the traditional approaches to A/AS teaching will not sit happily alongside the new institutional arrangements for delivering NVQs.

The fear that this will reduce the 'academic rigour' of 'A' level qualifications are not well founded. An outcome model will make it possible to define what academic rigour means. It will also be possible to specify the content and intellectual demands in relation to the needs of higher education and higher level NVQs. Experience with NVQs, suggests that comprehensive assessment and the need to reach the required standards in all areas, makes such qualifications more demanding and rigorous compared to those based upon choice and pass marks which they have replaced.

16   Implications for Higher Education

Higher education encompasses a wide range of provision. It is defined in respect of the 'academic' standard of a university degree and post graduate degrees. It is higher than A/AS levels and within the new NVQ framework, higher than level 3, although the latter criterion is less clear cut.

Degrees themselves vary widely in respect of their professional relevance and relationship to competence as defined in this book. Some degrees are linked closely to professional requirements (eg veterinary surgery, dentistry) others partially (eg psychology, economics) and yet others not at all in respect of content but only in respect of a general academic standard (eg classics, philosophy). Degrees, even when closely linked to a profession, tend to be based on a body of knowledge and theory, and treated as academic disciplines to be pursued for the purpose of intellectual development, rather than training in preparation for later professional practice. This is reflected in the culture and value systems which surround higher education. The further development of the discipline through research and analysis are normally the predominant concerns of providers of higher education, and profoundly influence the way in which subjects are taught.

Higher education, as we have suggested earlier, has a disproportionately large affect on education in schools, which often appears to be designed as a preparation for entry into higher education, although only a minority of young people actually do so.

This book does not attempt to evaluate the merits of the different objectives pursued within higher education, but it does suggest that it would be helpful to clarify such objectives. The outcomes pursued by any programme of study ought to be clear to both those providing the programme and the prospective students (learners). There is little doubt that many students embark on degree courses with very little idea of what is to be offered and to what it might lead.

There are in fact already signs of higher education institutions beginning to address these issues. A number of university and polytechnic departments are trying to state the aims of their degrees in the form of outcomes in a project co-ordinated by UDACE.[2] The Council for National Academic Awards (CNAA) is exploring competence based approaches to specifying degree requirements. They already operate the Credit Accumulation and Transfer Scheme (CATS) which is rapidly gaining in popularity. A prerequisite is the restructuring of degrees into component units. The CATS also recognises prior achievements gained through experience in employment as unit-credits towards a degree. The Open University, which already offers degrees in the form of units, is looking seriously at specifying unit requirements in the form of learning outcomes rather than programme inputs. Although modular degrees are not yet normal practice, their numbers are growing.

The Enterprise Initiative, launched by the Training Agency in 1987, is an experiment to build 'enterprise skills' into degree courses. It shares some objectives with the Technical and Vocational Educational Initiative (TVEI), which has attempted to make education in schools, 14 to 18 years, more relevant to employment. The way the Enterprise Programme is implemented varies between different universities and polytechnics, but in some the approach is similar to the proposed core skill initiative in A/AS levels and NVQs. Where skills development is superimposed upon academic courses, it tends to lead to specifying the skills as outcomes, continuous assessment and unit credits.

There is a strong and growing lobby to increase participation in higher education. Britain lags behind its primary economic competitors in the numbers entering higher education. It is of course one facet of the more general phenomena considered earlier, that participation rates in education and training post 16 years are lower in all age groups and sectors compared with our primary economic competitors.

In his recent publication 'More Means Different' Sir Christopher Ball,[1] spells out the nature of the problem and makes a number of very useful recommendations for increasing participation in HE. But despite the title, the difference refers to the ways HE is packaged and offered to the students. He suggests using facilities more efficiently and cost-effectively by adopting a four-term year, more part-time students, more open learning in the style of the Open University, and so on. What he does not contemplate is change in the structure of the provision which would greatly increase access and flexibility, and the potential for more cost-effective learning. This is surprising given the advent of NVQs in occupational and professional training and the introduction of the National Curriculum into schools. If these new approaches take root it is difficult to imagine they will not have an impact on higher education.

There seems little doubt that the role and form of higher education will be issues that are debated throughout the 1990s. The relationship between higher education and the development of professional competence is explored in Chapter 18.

17 Implications for Individuals: The Autonomous Learner

The new education and training model places the learner at the centre of the system. The learner is regarded as the client and the model is designed to provide him or her with more control over the process of learning and assessment.

Information Sources

Prospective learners will be provided with far more exact information on the functions performed in occupations and professions. They will be able to access this information at any level of detail, from general statements to very precise specifications (elements of competence) and even the standards of performance required in employment (performance criteria). The NVQ database provides a wealth of information on occupations which has never been available before, and is organised to be readily accessible through a variety of routes.

Learners will also be able to explore the qualifications and units on offer, classified within the NVQ framework to clarify their relationship to each other. As qualifications will be presented in terms of employment functions their relation to occupational and professional requirements will be clear. It is also anticipated that qualifications and units within the database will soon be linked directly to information on the availability of related courses, programmes, work experience placements and open learning materials. Given open access to information and professional guidance where required, individuals will be much better placed to make realistic education and career choices.

Action Plans

Action planning will give individuals the opportunity to negotiate the content of the programme of learning they wish to follow. Within the constraints of the opportunities available they will also be able to choose the modes of learning (eg formal courses, open learning, work experience), the time at which they study or practise their skills and the period over which they schedule their programme.

Knowing the Outcomes Required

Students and trainees will have complete access to the statements of competence, the precise outcomes they are expected to achieve, including the standards by which they will be assessed. This will give learners a degree of control over their own learning which has not been possible with traditional courses and examinations. Learners will be much better placed to evaluate their own progress and know when they have reached the required standard. They will be able to request assessment when they are ready and will be in a position to discuss and question assessment decisions. If the performance of a candidate falls short of the standards in some respects the precise reason can be explained to the candidate, if it is not obvious to them already.

Having outcomes and standards which are open and accessible to learners as well as trainers, takes the mystique out of assessment, and much of the threat. The fact that assessment decisions will not normally be based on a single performance but aggregated evidence, collected over time, also reduces the stress associated with one-off tests and examinations.

When assessment decisions are based upon a combination of evidence collected over time and possibly from different sources the concept of 'failure' as in one-off tests or examinations is no longer relevant. It is assumed that if learners have not yet reached the required standard in the competence being assessed, or they have not yet demonstrated sufficient evidence to satisfy the assessor, that they w.'l continue until they do. The concept of failure is replaced by 'not yet up to standard'. The distinction is more than semantic and recognises the true nature of the process of learning.

Increased Opportunities for Learning

The model assumes that learners will have far more opportunities and encouragement to develop their skills. Ideally, continuing learning will become a natural part of life and employment. Companies, like colleges and training institutions, will becomes centres of learning.

Learning will be tailored to suit the ability and opportunities of the individual. As learning will be largely controlled by learners, they will progress at their own pace. Some will need a lot of support and others will need very little.

The unit credit system will enable learners to select and design their own programmes. Gaining credit for relatively small achievements, and accumulating credits, will provide an incentive to persevere. The individual's National Record will bring together the various phases of the learning cycle — prior achievements, action planning, continuous assessment, and credits and qualifications achieved. It will also symbolise for the holder his or her participation in the national system.

In summary, free and readily available information, both of the national system and the detailed requirements of any qualification or training opportunity, provides individuals with opportunity and choice. Together with the openness of the learning targets and the standards for assessment, learners will have a high degree of control of their own learning. If this is combined with far more opportunities and encouragement for people to improve their competence, it should lead to significantly higher participation rates in education and training.

Part Three
Outstanding Issues

Part Three discusses related issues which have yet to be resolved and the ideas put forward are naturally more speculative and less well developed than in the previous chapters.

18   The Problem of Knowledge

The place of knowledge in an outcome-led system of education and training, as implied by NVQs, has recently emerged as a major issue. The term 'knowledge' is used in the broad sense to include the understanding of concepts, principles, theories, and relationships — in fact all the cognitive structures which underpin competent performance. In simpler language we might say we are here concerned with what people need in their heads to perform effectively with their hands, feet, voice, eyes, and so on.

A distinction is normally made between knowledge and the skills which also underpin competent performance. Skills can only be demonstrated through their application in performance (doing something), while knowledge can be elicited through the more abstract means of conversation, questioning and writing. The distinction becomes less clear when we consider cognitive skills (e.g. problem solving skills, perceptual skills) but skills refer to a process which leads to an outcome, while knowledge may be elicited as an abstraction from behaviour (e.g. facts, principles, theories).

The early arguments within the competence movement went something like this. If a person performs competently we need not be concerned with what he or she knows. Any knowledge the individual requires can be inferred from their performance. This 'black box' approach has considerable appeal but it does assume that it is possible and practicable to assess the required performance to attest to the competence.

As we have seen in earlier chapters, the assessment of competence is based directly on the elements of competence and their associated performance criteria. But we have also noted that more recent formulations of elements include range statements which emphasise that competence is defined in NVQs as being able to practise over a range of contexts or situations.

The above argument, that the assessment of performance is all that is required, would be sustainable if it was practicable to assess performance over the range to which an element of competence applies. In practice this is seldom possible, especially at higher levels within the NVQ framework where the potential range of application is considerable.

Evidence and Inferences of Transfer

Assessment in NVQs is conceived as the collection of evidence and the evaluation of that evidence against performance criteria. Emphasis is placed on the need for performance evidence, where possible under operational conditions in a normal work environment. But practical constraints normally limit such demonstrations to one context, such as one job in a particular organization, with perhaps a limited range of customers, clients, products or whatever the salient variables are within the element of competence.

The assessment issue which is raised is whether the evidence gathered from observable demonstrations is sufficient to attest to competence over the required range. If variation in practice is small between different contexts, demonstration in one context may be sufficient. This, for example, is the case with the driving test, where for practical purposes driving one car over a limited range of road conditions, and demonstrating the basic manoeuvres for 25 minutes to the required standards, is accepted for the award of a certificate of competence (and licence). With a driving licence one can drive any automobile, within a specified range, under any conditions in almost any country in the world. (This is the range statement for driving.) The assumption which is made, presumably, is that the variation in driving competence is relatively small between vehicles and road conditions such that transfer from one car to another can be reasonably inferred.

This example shows that the assessment makes assumptions about skill transfer, in order to decide what inferences to draw about performance in other contexts, from the evidence of competence presented in the first context. One factor which would seem significant to skill transfer is the variation in performance required between contexts. If, for example, the function specified by an element of competence could be achieved by applying the same procedure, irrespective of context, transfer between contexts might reasonably be assumed. If, on the other hand variations between contexts resulted in significant variation in performance requirements then transfer would not be a straightforward matter.

There are two basic approaches to assessing transferability of competence, other than checking performance in every possible context. The first is to anticipate the main variations which are likely to occur and ensure individuals know how to vary their performance according to the circumstances they meet. The second approach is to treat each new context as a problem which has to be diagnosed to determine what performance is required, drawing upon the individual's repertoire of skill and knowledge. The second approach assumes an understanding of the principles which underlie the activity in order to determine the most appropriate response. The two approaches are, of course, not mutually exclusive but somewhat different ways of looking at the same problem.

Coping with variation, as opposed to performing routine and proceduralized functions, provides a primary distinction between low level and high level occupations in the NVQ framework. In particular, coping with variation which cannot be anticipated is a characteristic of the most demanding jobs, at the forefront of development and innovation in a profession.

Thus we need to assess knowledge in NVQs to cope with variation in practice which cannot be assessed though performance demonstrations. Within a competence-base model of qualifications there is no justification for assessing knowledge for its own sake but only for its contribution to competent performance.

To attest to a candidate's competence in respect of an element, assessments of performance are always required in at least one context or set of conditions. If demonstrations occur in different contexts and conditions as part of the candidate's employment or training, then the additional evidence of performance should be collected to enable a more comprehensive assessment to be made. But for most assessment decisions, particularly those at higher and professional levels, the sum of the performance evidence is unlikely to be sufficient to ensure that the candidate could cope with future variations which might occur. This is where demonstrations of performance need to be supplemented by assessments of knowledge. The assessment decision should be made on the sum of performance plus supplementary evidence.

This approach to assessment has advantages over that of most traditional qualifications, in that it links knowledge assessments directly to competent performance. Two points may be made: (1) knowledge is required, in the context of practising an occupation or profession, not as an end in itself, but to ensure competent performance; and (2) knowledge is required to facilitate transfer of skills.

Earlier I outlined two approaches to transfer; they suggest the assessment of knowledge should concentrate on:

(a) the knowledge of the variation in circumstances that might be expected and how practices and procedures should be modified to meet different circumstances, over the range which is expected;
(b) an understanding of the principles or theory which explain the nature of the function or activity to be assessed.

How much evidence is sufficient reasonably to ensure that a candidate can perform competently in the required range of situations is an issue which can only be resolved through empirical research. In assessment for NVQs, it is suggested that the evidence should be gathered from:

— performance demonstrations in at least one context;
— additional performance demonstrations in varied contexts, if these occur naturally as part of the candidate's employment or are

required in training. (Otherwise a range of performance demonstrations for the purpose of assessment could only be justified for
elements where the cost of errors in assessment is very high);
— questioning to ensure understanding of the principles to explain the
nature of the activity and performance required;
— questioning to ensure knowledge of variation in response required in
relation to main variations in situations which might be presented.

The assessment decision is made on the accumulation of evidence from these
different categories. If there is a considerable volume of performance
evidence, the need for additional evidence from questioning would be cor-
respondingly less.

It will be recognised that there can be no certainty of predictions about
future performance in different contexts, or even repeated performance in the
same context. One can only increase the probability by ensuring the candidate has performed competently in similar situations and possesses relevant
supplementary knowledge to cope with others. In general the greater the
evidence available the higher will be the probability of predicting future
competent performance over the required range.

The Provision of Education and Training

The above analysis relates to assessment. This is because in the NVQ model
the statement of competence, and what is assessed, will set the target for
what is learnt. Thus to meet the assessment criteria set for an element, the
programme of learning should include opportunity to practise in one or more
contexts, opportunity to gain a knowledge of the underlying principles
governing the performance, plus knowledge of the variation that could occur
and how to modify performance accordingly.

This has direct implications for methods of teaching or how learning
should be facilitated. It indicates, for example, that it would be good practice
to question learners as they acquire skills and perform activities, on why they
are performing in a particular way. Why are particular methods, procedures
and strategies used? Such questioning would make students think about the
general principles which underly their performance. Learners could also be
encouraged to think about variations that are likely to occur and the implications of such variation for performance. If this style of teaching and learning
were adopted it would not only develop a more thoughtful approach to the
acquisition of skills, methods and procedures, it would encourage learners to
think about how their performance could be improved.

As continuous assessment will become the normal practice in NVQs,
and in the National Curriculum, questioning during the process of learning
which elicits the evidence of the required knowledge, can be accumulated for
the purpose of summative assessment for the award of the qualification. Some

more formal checks may also be required, but much more extensive evidence can be accumulated during continuous assessment, possibly over a period of years, than would be practicable in any formal assessments (examinations). A danger of formal tests and examinations is that the assessment of knowledge tends to be separated from the performance which it underpins. The continuous assessment of knowledge for summative purposes would have the added advantage of steering the learning provision in the direction indicated above and provide better integration between the acquisition of knowledge and the performance to which it relates.

Context in which Knowledge is Assessed

This raises a practical issue which needs to be addressed in assessment for NVQs. The knowledge which underpins one element of competence may also be relevant to many other elements. Some of the principles, theories and practices may be common to a wide range of activity and generally underpin the occupation or profession rather than any one element. In many areas, particularly at the higher levels of competence, there is a related body of knowledge and theory which underpins a wide range of competent performance. This body of knowledge would normally have its own internal coherence which should be acquired and understood by students. It would not be appropriate to perceive it, and assess it, simply in relation to elements of competence. A university degree, even a professionally recognised degree (eg medicine, law), is perceived as a form of intellectual development, an educational experience which has value in its own right even if one does not go on to practise professionally in the area to which it relates.

The NVQ model is conceived in terms of the close *integration* of practice and theory which implies integrated assessment and learning. Following the NVQ model would lead to the assessment of knowledge in respect of each element, where it is relevant to practice. There is thus a danger of assessing the same knowledge base in respect of different elements, possibly leading to over assessment. Nevertheless, simply to assess (and teach) them separately will fail to make the links between theory and practice which are so crucial for competent performance. Some compromise between these two approaches must be found.

The relationship between degrees and professional competence is complex. In some, such as in dentistry or veterinary surgery, there is a direct relationship and it is unlikely that many would pursue these degrees as a general education without the intention of later practising in these fields. At the other end of the continuum there are degrees (eg Egyptology, classics) which have no relationship with any profession, save teaching in those areas. Some degrees, such as psychology, may be pursued as a general purpose degree or as the first step towards becoming a professional psychologist. Then there are degrees in subjects such as accountancy and information technology, which, although seemingly associated with a profession, are not necessary for entry to, or for success in, that profession. The routes to professional qualification could usefully be clarified. Not all degrees are of equal value, either as a general education or in preparation for a profession, or for both.

When the body of knowledge is taught separately from the practice of a profession it tends to become an end in itself, developing its own structure and priorities, with the result that it does not necessarily relate closely to practice. The more relevant knowledge and theory which actually underpins professional performance is often acquired in a somewhat ad hoc manner, largely through experience, when the individuals encounter real problems in practising the profession or doing a job.

In a research project carried out at Manchester University, Boreham (1989) studied the pharmacokinetic theory taught to first year medical students in what seemed to be a contained area of applied medical practice, namely how to determine the dosage of a drug for epilepsy. He then interviewed highly experienced clinicians who actually prescribed drugs for epileptic patients, to find out how they applied the theory. He found out that not only did they make little use of the theory but that there were many clinical situations in which it could not be applied. The way in which they actually determined the drug dosage was based upon a set of principles largely derived from their clinical experience. They agreed that the theory was of interest and possibly provided some insights into the nature of the problem, but it was not the basis of practice. This observation certainly coincides with my own experience in areas such as psychology, economics and, particularly, management.

Returning to the dilemma of assessing knowledge in relation to performance or as a body of knowledge largely separate from performance, the ideal solution is perhaps to do both. Where a coherent body of knowledge exists, and where it is also studied for reasons other than practising a related profession, there is justification for pursuing it separately. It will also no doubt be assessed separately. But this should not be regarded as sufficient evidence or as a direct substitute for assessing the relevant knowledge in relation to professional performance. It is critically important that learners can draw upon and relate the relevant aspects of knowledge when presented with problems and situations in their professional or occupational role. Failure to do so is one of the weaknesses in current professional and occupational training.

There are several reasons why people find it difficult to draw upon the body of knowledge and theory they have acquired in solving practical problems in their employment. Often the knowledge and theory are not directly relevant. When theory is developed separate from professional practice it takes on a life of its own with its somewhat different values, priorities, constructs and language. It tends to pursue lines of development and address problems of intellectual interest, rather than the problems identified in the practice of the profession, which are often considered rather mundane. Even when the theories are relevant, the connections with practice have often not been adequately established during training to facilitate their application.

An analysis of the knowledge which people actually draw upon, and need to draw upon, to perform competently, may not appear in what is taught as the body of knowledge underpinning a profession or occupation, or if it is covered, may not be accorded the priority it deserves. Competent professionals tend to acquire a set of guiding principles, of which they are often only partially conscious, derived largely from their experience. These may build upon 'academic' theories and knowledge or be only loosely related. While this is recognized in areas such as management, it also appears to be true in well established professions such as medicine.

In summary, it would seem necessary, to create qualifications which assess the knowledge required to underpin and extend competent performance, directly in relation to such performance. It is suggested that this should occur even if the knowledge is assessed separately as part of an academic discipline.

19 Issues for The Future

There are of course many issues to be resolved before the full potential of the model of education and training presented can be realized. It is perhaps useful to distinguish between those issues which are concerned with the further development of the model, the concepts, methods and frameworks, and those which are concerned with its implementation, such as institutional change, staff development, resourcing and so on.

Can all Outcomes be Specified?

The way in which the outcomes required of education and training are specified, which has been considered at various points in Part One, remains central to the model. The assumption is made that the outcomes sought in education and training can be pre-determined and stated. There is a growing body of evidence to suggest this is possible in occupational and professional areas where the outcome is competence to practise. The functions which need to be performed in these areas provide an obvious basis from which to start. There are external reference points outside the education and training system, namely in the world of employment, which determine what needs to be learned and the standards of performance required. It is presumably not contentious that an analysis of the requirements of employment provides a reasonable starting point for occupational and professional training.

Whether it is possible to encapsulate in a statement of competence all the facets of performance we wish to see in a fully competent employee or professional, is an issue which many critics raise. Earlier attempts to do so have often led to rather narrow task-based specifications of competence which limit the focus of learning. This problem is not peculiar to outcome-based learning; it is a criticism which may be levied at training generally, and many forms of education, in that it tends to be narrow, focusing only on the more tangible aspects of performance. Thus training has tended to concentrate on tasks, procedures and technical requirements, while neglecting communication and management skills. Education has focused on the acquisition of a body of knowledge, while neglecting its potential application and many aspects of personal development.

The dangers of a narrow specification of competence or outcome are now well recognised. The new competence-based movement is attempting to go back to fundamentals and look at what is really required for successful performance or the achievement of successful outcomes in any field of learning. If one faithfully interprets the nature of competent performance, the less tangible skills (including an awareness of context and appropriateness of different responses) will be included as part of the statement. There would appear to be no intrinsic reason why the specification of outcomes should be narrow. Outcomes are what one makes them. They will reflect one's concept and understanding of the nature of competence and behaviour.

Education is not targeted to the same degree as an occupation or profession. Educational outcomes are by definition more generic and diffuse. One learns to read and write, for example, to apply these skills in a very wide variety of contexts, in life generally including work. The external reference points, upon which to base learning outcomes are almost infinite. Nevertheless, standards can be set in the form of outcome statements as we have seen in the National Curriculum.

The standards set in education are to some extent arbitrary, in so far as they are not based upon specific requirements in the outside world but a whole variety of requirements.[1] Nevertheless, we have plenty of experience of what basic educational outcomes are needed, at least in the core areas, and a consensus on what should be included. If the outcomes are defined in a progressive framework such as the National Curriculum, students can be encouraged to progress as far as they are able. In addition, certain minimum levels can be set which relate to external requirements to cope with life and work at certain levels of employment.

The other feature of basic education is that it tends to develop what is described in the competence-based system as the skills, knowledge and understanding which underpin competence. General education does not, in most areas, prepare people to tackle directly the functions of employment or life in general, but provides a basis from which the specific aspects of competence can be rapidly acquired. In some areas of competence, the additional requirements are small, while in others they are considerable.

A major issue with respect to outcome-led models of education, particularly at higher levels, concerns the supposed restriction of freedom this imposes on learning. We must however distinguish here between the process of stating outcomes as the targets for learning and the freedom individuals have to select the targets at which they wish to aim. Within the NVQ framework the objective is to set out the competence requirements of all the significant employment functions in the form of units. Which subset of units an individual chooses to pursue is a separate issue. In general we should encourage the freedom to choose. For recognition in an occupation field, particular subsets will make up NVQs. But even within NVQs there will often be degrees of choice to be exercised.

Within general education, the specification of outcomes does not dictate which outcomes should be pursued. Prescriptions may subsequently be imposed, as in the National Curriculum, or not. Within any programme of study, any degree of choice can be maintained within the spectrum of outcomes that have been specified. Outcome statements can be created for all learning which is considered important or that people want. As we have seen earlier, the model which stems from outcome-based learning includes an individual action plan promoting individualized learning. It is also part of the model that the action plan should be negotiated between the learner and the providers of education and training. Choice is also assumed in the model in the modes of learning selected to achieve the outcomes. In these two respects, through greater choice of outcomes and modes of learning, there will be more freedom for the learner in the proposed system than exists.

The real issue is whether targeting learning on predetermined outcomes restricts other forms of learning which otherwise might occur, and if so, what are these aspects of learning which might be neglected? These concerns stem partly from one's conception of what can or cannot be encapsulated in outcome statements. Current initiatives are specifying process skills in, for example, problem solving. These will certainly include aspects of what would normally be regarded as creativity.

If an objective of a programme of learning was to generate original solutions to a problem, there is no reason why this should not be stated as an outcome. Criteria could also be set on how originality would be judged. Outcomes do not need to state the solution but only the nature of the solution and the criteria which the solution must meet.

If an objective of a programme of learning was to develop creative writing or designs, these objectives could also be formulated as outcome statements. The criteria by which a poem or a short story is to be assessed can be stated so that the student knows what creative writing means. If this cannot be done it raises serious issues for both the assessment and development of such objectives.

There is also the belief among some educationalists that learners should pursue their inclinations and curiosity, unconstrained by pre-determined objectives. Certainly curiosity is a great motivator, and when it exists one would not wish to curb this form of learning. In my own experience curiosity is most often stimulated when one is tackling a real problem or pursuing targeted learning. If the issue is one of not having the time to pursue one's learning inclinations, in an outcome-based learning programme, one could perhaps build in a proportion of the programme as initially unprescribed or prescribed as 'original contributions related to the subject of this programme'. Individual action planning, of course, allows flexibility to review and revise targets as one progresses through the plan.

If it is argued, as it often is, that one cannot specify the outcomes one wants to achieve in a programme of learning, this raises serious problems of how to design the programme. The view is associated with another which is prevalent in higher education, that all learning is 'good' and it does not matter too much what you learn. This stems from the belief that what is important is the process of learning rather than the specific content or subject. This is reasonable in that the primary objective of much education might be the development of generic or process skills, including learning how to learn. The core skill initiative described in chapter 11 is intended to promote this objective. But if the development of such skills is seen as a primary objective, it should be made explicit by spelling out the skills as outcomes to be achieved. Their development should not be left to chance. It is perfectly feasible to specify such skills as outcomes in order to promote their development and to assess whether they have been achieved.

The premise put forward here is that all formal learning (that which goes on in the education and training system) and much informal learning would be more effective if targeted on specified outcomes. We need to know far more about the best form in which to state the outcomes but the methodology for doing so is developing rapidly. The other advantages which result, with respect to opening access to education, are presumably not disputed.

What Sort of Outcomes?

The concept of competence, reviewed in chapter 4, will remain a continuing issue of debate. The problem is not new to competence-based education and training, but the issue has been more clearly exposed by the need to make the outcomes quite explicit. A feature of the move towards outcomes, is that fundamental questions on content and forms of learning, which have been somewhat obscured by the apparatus of examinations and curriculum, are being clearly exposed and addressed.

The process of exposing the objectives of higher education, and the debate which surrounds it will be most illuminating. So much is currently hidden behind woolly concepts such as 'the maintenance of rigorous standards' and 'intellectual demands' that it is difficult to discuss its role and function, and consequently to what extent they are effectively achieved.

Learning and Transfer

The whole process of education and training makes implicit assumptions about the transfer or generalizability of skills and knowledge from the context in which learning takes place to other contexts where it might subsequently be applied or required. Some of the assumptions made about transferability are not well founded, for example, many recent studies have shown that arithmetical operations taught and acquired devoid of context (i.e.

adding, multiplying figures on paper), do not necessarily transfer to practical problems which require the same operations. Nor does the successful application in one context (eg adding up on the dart board) necessarily transfer to other contexts.

We need to know a great deal more about the mechanisms of transfer and how they relate to the process of learning. The issues are greatly complicated by the variation between individuals. While some individuals find little difficulty in transferring skills other clearly do.

Models of Learning and Behaviour

It has become apparent in addressing the issue of what evidence is sufficient in assessment to infer competence and, more particularly, what learning opportunities most effectively develop competence, that a variety of assumptions about the process of learning and behaviour must be made. We need to develop more sophisticated models of what underpins competent performance. The relationship between knowledge, skills and competent performance are not well understood. Cognitive skills, process skills and core skills are different ways of conceptualizing those seemingly basic skills which underpin most purposeful behaviour. When one digs into the subject, one recognizes that education and training is a pretty hit-and-miss affair and often remarkably inefficient. This has always been the case and our expectations are so low that the situation is tolerated.

These issues are so central, both to our personal fulfilment in life and the economic success of the country, which further effects our personal fulfilment, that it is surprising that we do not take them more seriously.

Although difficult to prove, it also seems a reasonable hypothesis that alienation from the education system, combined with consequent poor employment opportunities, contributes to the rise in crime and hooliganism among young people today. Even if a causal connection does not exist, it would seem probable that a more positive attitude to education among young people would ameliorate the problem.

Debates on education, even among the professionals in the field, tend to be so value laden and politicised that it is difficult to conduct a rational analysis, or carry out the research which is required to provide a better understanding of the processes involved.

Attitudinal and Institutional Change

As indicated in chapters 13–17, the introduction of the new model has enormous implications for, not only institutional arrangements, but even people's conception of education and training. The technical problems, important as they are, pale into insignificance beside the scale of the change required in companies, schools and colleges to establish a 'learning society'. Yet the process has already begun and has widespread support in many quarters. It will become easier when we have good models for others to see. We can take heart perhaps when we see the scale and speed of change which has taken place in Eastern Europe recently, and which few people would have considered possible.

The time is right for change. The problems with the current education and training provision have been identified and concern has been growing, particularly among employers, with the extent to which we lag behind other industrialised countries. People are searching for a way forward.

20   Summary and Conclusions

The previous chapters, while dealing primarily with the model of education and training which stems from NVQs, have looked briefly at related initiatives in other parts of the education system, namely the National Curriculum, A/AS levels and higher education. It is assumed that these will be the major components of the national provision of education and training in the future. This chapter attempts to draw together the threads and illustrate what an integrated provision for learning could look like.

Outcomes

The common feature, which will come as no surprise to readers by this time, would be that all forms of learning provision would be stated in terms of outcomes. Thus there would be predetermined statements in the form of competences or attainments which serve as targets and guide the course of learning. The statements also form the basis of assessment and recognition of achievement.

There will be rules (criteria) governing the form of statements. These will be linguistic conventions to aid the communication on the meaning of statements. There are also what have been described as technical requirements to ensure that the statements meet the need for assessment, but this is simply another way of saying that statements must accurately communicate their intent. For accurate communication of the outcomes of competence and attainment, a precision in the use of language in such statements will need to be established, approaching that of a science. The overall model stands or falls on how effectively we can state competence and attainment. But if we cannot it raises fundamental issues for education and training, irrespective of the model used. If you cannot say what you require, how can you develop it and how do you know when you have achieved it?

The Concepts of Competence and Attainment

Outcome-led models of education and training force a fundamental review of the objectives of education and training by making the objectives explicit. This would seem an entirely desirable, if somewhat demanding, discipline to impose.

The process has already generated a debate in vocational education about the concept of competence, as reflected in NVQs. For example, how broad or narrow should it be? To what extent should it promote the development of process skills or core skills as opposed to, or in addition to, task specific skills? How far should we build in flexibility and adaptability? We all know the prevailing rhetoric on these issues but we need to obtain a consensus on what we can realistically achieve and at what cost. How do we balance the short term needs of employers with the longer term needs of individuals and the nation?

To date the public debate surrounding the National Curriculum has been more narrowly focused, although similar issues have emerged in the approaches adopted in specifying statements of attainment in subjects such as History. Few people have asked why History is included at all in the National Curriculum. (I am not suggestion it should not be included but I think the question should be asked and answered). The debate on core skills raises the question of why the National Curriculum is based on subjects in preference to cross-curricular themes. Actually the inclusion of Science and Technology as two of the ten National Curriculum 'subjects' breaks new ground compared to the normal divisions in GCE and now GCSE.

Assessment

Assessment is being brought into the real world and de-mystified within the new model of education and training. We shall, I hope, see the demise of the last minute swotting of information soon to be forgotten for examinations. We shall not need to play those games in the future — games which few enjoy and where the majority finish up losers. Assessment will be open (the word 'transparent' is coming into vogue when what is meant is simply 'explicit' — able to be seen, rather than seen through). What is assessed and the standards of performance required are open to both the assessor and the candidate alike. Learners will be able to make judgements about their own performance which will have implications for their own learning. Self-assessment will become an important component in learning. It will also often contribute to and initiate assessment by tutors and supervisors.

Assessment will be continuous, normally integrated with the process of learning. There will be a much more harmonious relationship between learning, formative assessment, and summative assessment (providing evidence of achievement) in which both learners and tutors participate as required. Assessment will be seen as natural and helpful, rather than threatening and sometimes a distraction from real learning as in traditional models.

Assessment will be far more thorough, it will focus on what needs to be assessed and will cover more systematically a far wider range of outcomes than can be achieved by traditional methods. As a consequence it will be more valid.

The prevailing ethos, surrounded by much psychometric mystique, that 'rigour' and 'standards' can only be obtained by externally set examinations where every candidate is subjected to the same treatment, even if it is only marginally relevant, must be questioned. (See also Appendix 'D').

Learning

As we have seen in earlier chapters a primary aim of the new model is to open access to learning to far more people. The new approach encourages learning in a wide range of locations and by different methods. By recognising the skills and knowledge people already have, it will raise their confidence and give them a flying start in any new programme they embark upon. The targets for learning will be more relevant and relate more to the needs of individuals. Learning will not be equated in the minds of people with 'academic', 'classrooms', 'boredom' and 'failure'.

Learner-Led

The model is designed to promote learning and to maximise efficiency in the process of learning. There are many features which contribute to this, some of which we have already touched upon above. They include:

— the effective provision of information and guidance where required, on the qualifications, units and attainment targets on offer in any area, and how they are related within a progressive framework. This is made possible by the creation of a coherent national framework for learning and computerized databases which allow ready access to vast stores of information. Neither of these features have been available in the past;
— recognition of prior achievements — the base-line which future learning builds upon — recognizes the uniqueness of the learner;
— the development of individual action plans, which allows considerably more choice and participation by the learner in the targets they choose to pursue in any course or programme. Flexibility and choice is considerably enhanced by unit-based qualifications and modular delivery. There will also be choice in the modes and timing of

learning, and the duration of programmes, within what can be accommodated by providers. These features will perhaps be more evident in the post-school provision, where adults will tailor their action plans to fit in with the rest of their lives. Within schools pre-16, the National Curriculum will largely dictate the targets of learning, but there will be increasing choice through individualised learning with projects and assignments and progress at different speeds through the provision;

— clear understanding by learners of what they are expected to learn (as set out in statements of attainment or competence) and the performance levels by which they will be assessed, will give them a degree of control over the process which has not been a feature of traditional programmes;

— the above allows self-assessment and participation in summative assessment through a dialogue with the assessor on what the learner has demonstrated they know and can do.

A Coherent Framework

By adopting common structures (ie statements of outcome) for different forms of education and training provision we have, for the first time, the possibility of relating different programmes, qualifications and forms of provision. The skills which are common between occupations can be recognised. The relevance of the skills and knowledge gained in schools to vocational and professional competence can be identified. This will make possible a much smoother transition from school or university to vocational and professional training.

We considered early in the book the problems and inefficiencies caused by the proliferation of different training initiatives in recent years. With a single national framework, each new initiative would select its range of outcomes from the framework, and would be immediately recognisable and understood. Whatever course they choose, individuals would be able to gain nationally recognized credits and qualifications. They would also be able to relate their achievements to what they had acquired previously and to what they might do subsequently. Each new YTS, ET or TOPS, would simply be different mechanisms of funding, aimed at different populations, to meet short term skills shortages or employment gaps in a person's career. All programmes would feed the same national framework of standards or outcomes.

The Process of Learning

An assumption is often made that because NVQs, and the broader models described here, are defined only by their outcomes that the proponents of such approaches to education and training are not concerned with the process of learning. In one sense this is true, in so far as competence and attainment is recognized irrespective of the process by which it is acquired. In another sense it is far from true.

The overall model is designed to promote learning. It incorporates many features which make learning more attractive and easier to access. The emphasis on performance and attainment encourages more active and participative learning.

What the model does not do is assume there is only one way to learn or even that there is necessarily a best way. It recognizes individual differences and individual preferences and opportunities. Above all it does not prescribe the form of learning.

Glossary of Terms

Although the primary concepts on which the model is constructed are explained and defined in the text, it may be useful to have concise definitions in one place. This is the place. It will be appreciated that everyday words like 'standard' and 'unit' have very specific meanings when used in this book.

ACHIEVEMENT, the outcome of learning, the acquisition of competence, skill or knowledge.

ACCREDITATION OF PRIOR LEARNING, certificating competence on the basis of evidence from past achievements, often supplemented by current assessments. Sometimes used in a wider sense to include counselling, helping people to recognise the significance of their experience as a prelude to assessment and accreditation, and providing guidance and action planning following such accreditation (also referred to as 'accreditation of prior achievement').

ASSESSMENT (for CERTIFICATION), the process of collecting evidence and making judgements on whether the evidence meets the standards set (by performance criteria) and whether the evidence is sufficient to attest to competence or attainment.

ATTAINMENT TARGETS, the broad objectives specified in a [National Curriculum] subject, setting out the knowledge, skills and understanding pulils are expected to acquire.

BREADTH, a global term which is applied to qualifications, statements of competence, and thereby education and training, to refer to the coverage of competence or attainment, the extent to which it promotes underpinning knowledge and skills and as a result of these and/or by other means, promotes adaptability and transferability.

CERTIFICATE, a document issued to an individual by an awarding body, formally attesting to achievement or attainment (e.g. of an NVQ, units of competence, other qualifications or achievements).

COMPETENCE, the ability to perform to recognised standards (what this entails is a matter of continuing debate, see chapter 3)

CORE SKILLS, skills (or facets of skill) which underpin, and are common to, a wide range of competent performance. The acquisition of such skills is believed to facilitate transfer to performance in a wide range of functions and situations.

CREDIT, formal recognition of achievement through certification. In particular, the recognition of units or components of qualifications.

CREDIT ACCUMULATION, the general process by which separate components of a qualification system can be separately achieved and certificated, allowing the accumulation of such achievements over time.

CREDIT TRANSFER, the recognition of a credit gained in one qualification, or system of qualifications, as satisfying some or all of the requirements of a different qualification, or system of qualifications. It alleviates the need for repeating assessments (and possibly training) for the award, or that part of the award, for which recognition is given in the second qualification or system.

ELEMENT OF COMPETENCE (sometimes referred to as just 'ELEMENT'), the smallest and most precise specification of competence within an NVQ statement of competence. A component part of a unit of competence.

FORMATIVE ASSESSMENT, assessment to facilitate the process of learning; assessment which is fedback to learners including diagnosis of further learning requirements. (May be informal and locally determined.)

FUNCTION, description of an activity by reference to its purpose and outcome.

FUNCTIONAL ANALYSIS, a method of analysing the competence requirements in an area (eg industry, occupation, organisation) according to functions which need to be carried out to fulfil its overall purpose.

INDUSTRY LEAD BODY (ILB), (or LEAD BODY), an institution or group formally recognised as having responsibility for setting standards (more precisely, determining the statements of competence) within a given area of competence.

INDIVIDUAL ACTION PLAN, a plan which sets out learning targets and learning opportunities to be provided, negotiated between learner and provider, tailored to meet the needs of an individual, taking into account their prior achievements. The targets are stated, where appropriate, as the outcomes specified in units and attainment targets in qualifications.

JOB, the unique work role or group of functions which is/are carried out by an individual in employment.

JOB CATEGORY, a group of jobs encompassing similar functions.

KNOWLEDGE, the 'know-how' or cognitive component which underpins competence or attainment, which may include facts, theories, principles, conceptual frameworks etc. It subsumes 'understanding'. May be elicited through questioning techniques.

LEARNING, the process of acquiring skills, knowledge, and/or competence.

NATIONAL VOCATIONAL QUALIFICATION (or NVQ), a qualification which is accredited by NCVQ and allocated to a place within the NVQ framework. NVQs are required to meet specified criteria for accreditation (see NVQ criteria).

NVQ CRITERIA, the criteria published by NCVQ which NVQs are expected to meet for accreditation. They provide the criteria for the design of NVQs, the primary features of which are a statement of competence and open access to assessment.

NVQ FRAMEWORK, the national system of classifying NVQs according to area of competence and level.

NATIONAL CURRICULUM, the national system of classifying attainment targets and statements of attainment, by subject and levels. The required education provision for school children aged 5 to 16 years in state schools.

NATIONAL RECORD OF VOCATIONAL ACHIEVEMENT, a file published by NCVQ encompassing a system of prior records, action planning, continuous assessment recording and certificates, deriving from the national system of credit accumulation and transfer.

NATIONAL SYSTEM OF CREDIT ACCUMULATION AND TRANS-FER, the system which is being created by a consortium of awarding bodies, co-ordinated by NCVQ, in which vocational qualifications will be offered as a number of units for separate assessment, recording and certification. It includes arrangements for credit accumulation, through the National Record of Vocational Achievement, and the recognition of units awarded by one body by the others.

NCVQ DATABASE, a computerised database of NVQs and other vocational qualifications of the major national awarding bodies, containing detailed information of their units, elements, performance criteria and assessment methods, available for public access.

OCCUPATION, a defined area of competence which is relevant to performance in a range of jobs in different companies and locations, and often different industries.

PERFORMANCE CRITERIA, the criteria which define the standard required in the performance of an element of competence.

PROFESSION, a high level occupation which is characterised by a code of conduct and values, providing identity, normally derived through membership of a professional body.

PROGRESSION, the development or accumulation of competence or attainment by an individual through successive learning opportunities (programmes/courses/qualifications/experiences) in a systematic manner. Also the related advancement in an individual's career through successive jobs.

RANGE (or RANGE STATEMENT or RANGE OF APPLICATION), an addition to an element of competence which indicates the range of application of the element. Lists primary sources of variation in conditions and contexts in which performance may be required.

RECORD OF ACHIEVEMENT, either a document recording achievement like a certificate or a 'file' for recording and maintaining a variety of achievements and experiences. May also include other features.

SKILLS, the 'performance' component which underpins competence. Distinguished from competence by being more fundamental and frequently common to a variety of different competences. They may also be demonstrated, divorced from context, unlike competence. Skills may be manual or cognitive, or a combination of both.

SKILL TRANSFER, the ability to perform a new function competently, or with a reduction in learning time than would otherwise be required to achieve competence, as a result of the previous acquisition of a skill or skills in a different function or context. Particularly pertinent to core skills which are common and transferable to performance in a wide range of functions. (Can also be used to apply to transfer between contexts, rather than functions.)

STATEMENT OF COMPETENCE, a specification of the competence required in a given area. In NVQs this is set out in a prescribed format of title, units of competence, elements of competence and performance criteria.

STATEMENT OF ATTAINMENTS, the more precise objectives which make up an attainment target, defined at graduated levels of attainment.

STANDARDS, normally a short-hand term referring to statements of competence or components within such statements. A more precise concept of 'standard' is expressed by the performance criteria, within statements of competence (ie the standard of performance required by an element of competence).

UNIT OF COMPETENCE (sometimes referred to as just 'UNIT'), a primary sub-division of the NVQ statement of competence, representing a discrete aspect of competence. A unit is made up of elements of competence. Units are also offered for independent certification for credit accumulation and transfer.

UNIT-CREDIT, a credit, formally awarded by the issue of a certificate, based upon a unit of competence, within the national system of credit accumulation and transfer.

VERIFICATION, the process of monitoring carried out by an awarding body, or its representatives, to ensure that assessment is conducted faithfully (ie according to specified procedures or within specified criteria), for the purpose of certification.

Notes

1 Various writers have made similar points about education and training in the UK. For example:

> 'The sociological analysis of teaching is, furthermore usually undertaken with minimal reference to the learning outcomes for pupils which are themselves important sources of legitimation for teachers.' Esland (1971).

> 'Much work on the development of education and training for adults has concentrated on the content and process of learning rather than on its outcomes. This has tended to focus on syllabuses and courses as the starting point for the provision and required the student to adjust her or himself to an established curriculum and mode of delivery ... a greater emphasis on the outcomes of learning could help provide both more effective approaches to learning and widen participation.' (UDACE, 1990, p. 2).

2 This quotation is from the interim report of the CBI Task Force on Vocational Education and Training: 'Towards a skills revolution: a youth charter', July, 1989. The Task Force has become an influential new voice in education and training and the recommendations from its second report: 'Towards a Skills Revolution' are reproduced at Appendix 'B' of the book.

3 Quotation from 'Vocational and General Education in England' by Gerhard Lachenmann, in 'Vocational and General Education in Western Industrial Societies', editor Hermann Rohrs, 1988.

4 Burke (1985) discusses the relationship between teaching and learning:

Hirst (1971) has demonstrated that the concept of teaching is totally dependent on learning since the intention of all teaching activities is to bring about some learning. He goes on:

> If therefore a teacher spends the whole afternoon in activities the concern of which is not that his pupils should learn he cannot have been teaching at all. In these terms, it could be that quite a large number of professional teachers are, in fact, frauds most of their lives.

Illich (1971) also considers the relationship between teaching and learning in 'Deschooling Society'. Reviewing this immensely influential work, Merriman wrote:

> Illich, I believe, has done us a service in demonstrating the primacy of learning over schooling, and, as such its potential independence.

5 Cohen and Manion (1981), commenting on Hammersley (1977):

> The next dimension along which definition of the teacher role may vary is the degree of control over pupils and their learning which the teacher claims. (...) Teaching may also vary in the degree of control the teacher is required to exercise over what is to be learned, how, when and at what pace. He is careful to point out, however, that the polar opposite of teacher control, that is, absence of teacher control, does not mean chaos, but rather a corresponding increase in pupil control.

The wider issue of who controls knowledge was explored in Young (1971).

Stenhouse's (1975) observation that 'the school is teaching a content on which it has a lease rather than a possession' (p. 12) is here pertinent.

Eraut (1988) suggests that one of the major weaknesses in the development of learning design as educational technology has been 'a failure to develop learners' awareness and control of their own learning, what we now call their metacognition.'

6 Targeting on explicit outcomes is now widely recognised among the most highly regarded training organizations in industry, as evidenced in a first Leader in The Times Educational Supplement 15 June 1990, p. A.19:

Few people would deny that more needs to change before we have a thoroughly effective system and more reforms are under-way [in teacher training]. The industrial trainers [from B.P., I.B.M. and Lloyds Bank], hosted by HMI, were surprised that objectives in terms of outcomes were not set in advance: but the Department of Education and Science circular 24/89, published after their visit, sets sensible and clear objectives in terms of what students should be able to do after their training. Universities and colleges are currently taking them on board.

7 It is interesting to note Neave (1974) on this point:

Furthermore, children's interests are not likely to fit in with the official notion of education being academic, vocational or tech-nical. Indeed, the free schoolers have argued, the whole process of education is hampered by the artificial division into subjects of greater or lesser repute, a division which has little foundation other than in the minds of teachers.

Chapter 2

1 See 'Employment in the 90s', Department of Employment, HMSO (1988).
2 See Labour Party policy document: Investing in Britain's Future: Labour's programme for post-16 education and training (1990)
3 CBI Report of the Vocational Education and Training Task Force: 'Towards a Skills Revolution', 1989.
4 See TUC report 'Skills 2000', 1989.
5 See for most recent analysis 'Britain's real skill shortage, and what to do about it' by Sir John Cassels, 1990.
6 Note the opening paragraph in Holt (1969, p. 9):

Most children in school fail.

The Ordinary Level ('O' Level) General Certificate of education (GCE) was introduced in 1951. It was aimed at the top 20% of school pupils. Until 1975, each examining board awarded its own grades from 1–9, 1–6 being passes. After 1975, the grading system was changed to grades A–E in which D–E were failures. The General Certificate of Secondary Educa-tion (GCSE) awards on a seven point scale but, in practice, grades 1–3 are widely recognised as passes equivalent to A–C GCE. The majority of school children are therefore destined 'To fail' in their own perception and in the perception of parents, employers and their peers, whatever the 'official' definition of the situation.

If we design our education system for failure, by a cruel stroke of irony we cannot help but succeed in our aim. It is far more difficult, challenging and worthwhile to plan for success built on the success of achievable, valued outcomes.

Note Bloom (1971, p. 4) on this point:

> The most wasteful and destructive aspect of our present educational system is the set of expectations about student learning each teacher brings to the beginning of a new course or term. (...) Students quickly learn to act in accordance with them.... A pernicious self fulfilling prophecy has been created.

The Certificate of Secondary Education (CSE) (now superseded by the GCSE) was introduced in 1965 in an attempt to offer a school-leaving qualification to the top 60%. However, it lacked the status of the 'O' Level GCE (top grade CSE equivalent to grade C, GCE) and was soon widely perceived as a qualification for the less able, and therefore of very doubtful negotiable value.

7   'The New Training Initiative: Agenda for Action' (1981) published by the Manpower Services Commission and subsequently as a government White Paper provides the basic philosophy and the starting point for many of the initiatives which underpin the model presented in this book.

8   National standards were considered in an MSC paper, Jessup (1983): 'Developing national standards in the YTS core: feasibility of 'Standard Tasks', AGCS paper 83/37 (unpublished).

Chapter 3

1   Goffman (1959, p. 55) provides an interesting insight into the function of 'time serving' as part of the mystification process:

> Reinforcing these ideal impressions ('the sacred compatibility between the man and the job ... commonly fostered by members of the higher professions' but 'also found among the lesser ones') there is a kind of 'rhetoric of training' whereby labour unions, universities, trade associations and other licensing bodies require practitioners to absorb a mystical range and period of training, in part to maintain a monopoly, but in part to foster the impression that the licensed practitioner is someone who has been reconstituted by his learning experience and is now set apart from other men. Thus, one student suggests about pharmacists that they feel that the four year university course required for licence is 'good

for the profession' but that some admit that a few months training is all that is really needed. (Weinlein 1943) It may be added that the American Army during the Second World War innocently treated trades such as pharmacy and watch-repairing in such a purely instrumental way and trained efficient practitioners in five or six weeks to the horror of established members of these callings.

Verney (1945, and 1989 p. 362) provides another graphic example. During the War in occupied France, a Resistance group decided to print a newspaper; they purloined a complete printing press. Verney continues:

> The requisite plant once acquired, the next problem was the question of how to use it. A schoolmaster, a doctor, three young women students and a nurse resolved to learn the techniques and succeeded after forty hours of earnest efforts, though the professional man who had agreed to teach them had warned them they would need at least five or six months training.

2 David Hutchinson (1990) pp. 164–181 has written a chapter 'Students with special needs' specifically related to the introduction of NVQs. His introduction begins:

> The reform and rationalisation of the national system of vocational qualifications are likely to be of benefit to all students, especially students with special needs. The advantages of the new system of credit accumulation and the National Record of Vocational Achievement (NROVA) which merit attention as likely to be of particular benefit to students with special needs are:
>
> — Easier access to qualifications;
> — Units can be built up over time;
> — Students can be motivated by the immediate recognition of achievements;
> — Different parts of a learning programme and different modes of learning can be integrated;
> — More flexible learning programmes can be designed; A clear statement of the student's competence can be made in language familiar to an employer.

See also NCVQ Information Note No. 3: Access and Equal Opportunities in Relation to National Vocational Qualifications, London, NCVQ, 1988.

3 A more recent joint publication by the CBI and NCVQ (1990) considers the implication for NVQ levels of the targets set by the CBI in 'Towards

a skills revolution' (1989). It provides somewhat more insight into the nature of the levels and the functions they will serve.

Chapter 4

1 An analysis of various definitions of 'occupational competence' and how they have evolved in contained in 'Insufficient Evidence', the final report of the competency testing project by Lindsay Mitchell and Tommy Cuthbert, SCOTVEC, 1989, (pp.7 to 14 and Appendix 1: What is occupational competence ?)

Tuxworth (1989, pp. 10–25) provides an overview of historical development of competence based education and training, mainly in the USA.

See also Oates (1989 pp.187–189) for an observation on developments in the UK.
2 The CBI Task Force Report (1989b, pp.25–28) has been particularly influential in providing an employer view on the need for broad based NVQs. See also summary of CBI recommendations at Appendix B of this book.
3 The Job Competence Model (Mansfield and Mathews, 1985) conceives of competence as four inter-related components:

> task skills — the routine and largely technical components of an occupation
>
> contingency management skills — the skills to recognise and deal with irregularities and variances in the immediate working environment
>
> task management skills — the skills to manage a group of tasks and prioritize between them
>
> role/job environment skills — the skills to work with others and cope with environmental factors which are required to fulfil the wider role expectations.

It has been useful in emphasising that competence involves more than the task skills, which have been primarily the concern of training and assessment for qualifications in the past, but it needs further development to become operationalised in the methodology for specifying competence.

It is interesting to note the relationship between task management skills and what Bruner (1966, p. 6) sees as a significant aspect of intellectual development:

Intellectual development is marked by increasing capacity to deal with several alternatives simultaneously, to tend to several sequences during the same period of time and to allocate time and attention in a manner appropriate to those multiple demands.

NCVQ should also note as a factor in determining NVQ levels.

4 Note also NCVQ (1990e) p. 2:

The National Council aims to identify and enhance core skills in NVQs in order to ensure breadth in the statement of competence upon which they are based. In particular, it believes that the conscious development of the fundamental core skills will;
—enhance the transferability of competent performance between different context and occupations;
—help employees to respond flexibly to changing skill requirements;
—provide a basis for progression within the NVQ framework.

Chapter 5

1 The first recorded attempt to operationalise the 'new kinds of standards' proposed in the New Training Initiative (1981) may be traced to an internal MSC paper, Jessup (1983) in the context of assessing core skills.
2 Reproduced from 'Standards in clerical and administrative occupations: Managing Agents Guide to standard tasks', MSC, 1984.
3 See 'Caterbase Guidelines' by the Hotel and Catering Training Board, 1987.
4 The first recorded use of range statements was by Lindsay Mitchell of Barbara Shellbourne Development in 1988. See discussion in Mitchell (1989).
5 Currently the best description of functional analysis is contained in TA, DE (1989) 'Developing standards by reference to functions'.
6 Compiled from an unpublished report to NCVQ by Nick Boreham (1990) 'An investigation of methodological issues relating to specifying professional competence'.
7 The author is not unaware of some of the previous attempts to spell out the outcomes of learning in the form of behavioural objectives and the debate it has generated, going back to Bobbitt (1918), Charters (1924), Tyler (1949), Bloom (1956), Mager (1962) and so on. The model outlined in this book is differs in several significant respects.

Many previous initiatives have been limited in the conceptual model of learning upon which they are based. For example, Stenhouse (1975, pp.

70–83) only addressed the issue in relation to its implications for curriculum development, which was conceived as teaching in a classroom:

> 'In short, curriculum study should be grounded in the study of classrooms' (Stenhouse, 1975, p. 75)

> 'Rational curriculum planning must take account of the realities of classroom situations. It is not enough to be logical.' (Stenhouse, 1970, p. 78, reproduced in Stenhouse, 1975, p. 75)

The model presented here is based upon a more fundamental conception of learning, wherever it takes place. It sees the classroom as just one context. It also makes a very clear distinction between learning and teaching.

An important distinction between earlier outcome models and the current one is in the way assessment is conceived. A major concern of the critics of outcome approaches has been that only outcomes that could be easily assessed would be included, and that assessment was limited to existing psychometric and exam-based approaches. A crucial aspect of the new model is that assessment is regarded as the collection of evidence from any relevant source. The specification of outcomes should not be constrained by considerations of assessment. It is argued that any outcome that can be articulated clearly can also be assessed. Further, if it cannot be articulated it presents problems in fostering its development as well as assessment.

A further distinction is the way in which outcomes are conceived and specified. The functional approach now adopted does not limit the breadth of the outcome specified to the constructs of a psychological model of learning.

Chapter 6

1   The Training Agency, Department of Employment, has published a series of guidance notes on the process of setting standards, see TA, DE (1988a), (1988b) and (1989) in particular. See also NCVQ/TA (1990): Developing NVQs. Also note the TA publication 'Competence and Assessment', published three times a year, which includes relevant articles.
2   Reference from 'Establishing the NVQ Framework: critical Path to 1992' NCVQ (1990).

Chapter 7

1 Assessment is also seen as integral to the process of learning in the National Curriculum. Note 'The National Curriculum: Task Group on Assessment and Testing: A Report', Department of Education and Science and the Welsh Office, 1987, paragraph 3:

> 'Promoting children's learning is a principal aim of schools. Assessment lies at the heart of this process. It can provide a framework in which educational objectives may be set, and pupils' progress charted and expressed. It can yield a basis for planning the next educational steps in response to children's needs. By facilitating dialogue between teachers, it can enhance professional skills and help the school as a whole to strengthen learning across the curriculum and throughout its age range.'

2 The 'wash-back' effect of assessment upon the curriculum is so well known that it requires little comment here: 'what is taught is what is assessed.' What may be less well known (or remembered) are the clandestine strategies resorted to by students to limit their learning to what they think is likely to be assessed. Becker (1968), Becker and Geer (1958) and Becker *et al.* (1961) elaborate these painstaking and sometimes sophisticated strategies, which amount in Wood's (1983, p. 47 and p. 104) terms to 'survival strategies', as students strive to discern what it is relevant to learn and what it is possible to learn within the syllabus.

3 Stones (1966, pp. 251ff) substantiates this point in respect of detailed marking schemes, analytical and impression marking, limited coverage, predictability and question spotting, cramming, model answers for regurgitation, variability in marker's assessments, inconsistency and 'examination skills'.

Also note Ingenkamp (1977):

> 'More attention has been paid to the essay type examination than any other form of written examination. It has repeatedly been shown that assessment of the same composition can differ to such an extent that the entire grading range is covered' (Starch and Elliot, 1912, Lammerman, 1927, Hartog *et al.*, 1936, Sims, 1932).

It may come as a surprise that school examinations for pupils are a comparatively modern innovation in the history of education. It may be even more surprising to reflect on the original purpose of school examinations, which was to assess the effectiveness of teachers rather than pupils, Burke (1985, p. 80):

[The formative effect of Butler's development of the sixth form as a separate educational category] may be said to arise from a further innovation — his use of examinations. Previously, examinations had been used mainly as a devise for assessing the efficacy of masters by patrons and visitors. Butler appropriated their use as a means of assessing the performance of the boys, and at Shrewsbury he promoted the more able pupils not by age but by attainment. As a result of these pressures, under Butler Shrewsbury soon acquired a reputation for academic excellence as so many boys carried off scholarships to Oxford and Cambridge. The end result was that other public schools imitated his methods.

We thus see that the earliest use of pupil examination was directed to selection, based on a normative ideology which has coloured virtually all educational thinking until very recently.

4 See also Jessup (1985a) p. 40 and Jessup (1989) pp. 66–67 on problems with traditional approaches to assessment.

5 See also Burke and Jessup 'Disentangling validity from reliability, in (Ed) Nuttall, D., to be published.

6 Two major projects have been carried out to test and evaluate the feasibility of workbased assessment based upon elements of competence and performance criteria. Wood, R., Johnson, C., Blinkhorn, S., Anderson, S., and Hall, J. (1988) p. 144 concluded that:

workplace assessment is viable but it needs attention and support.

Miller, C, Hoggan, J, Pringle, S and West, G (1988) p. 348 stated in summary:

Regarding the feasibility and acceptability of observational assessment in the workplace, the project reported no significant constraints operating on feasibility and widespread acceptance of the desirability of this form of assessment.

7 In the debate on the feasibility of workplace assessment, insufficient attention has been paid to the distinction between the new approach based upon clearly defined standards and previous practices in which no such standards existed. Many judgements on the feasibility of workplace assessment are based on earlier subjective practices and various 'profiling' methods in the absence of criteria against which to base assessments. No claims are here made for the validity of workplace assessment unless judgements are made in respect of elements of competence and performance criteria.

8   See Mitchell and Cuthbert (1989) for description of 'extracted examples of work'.

Chapter 8

1   NCVQ Information Note No. 5 (1989b) Assessment in NVQs: use of evidence of prior achievement (APL) describes how APL fits into the NVQ assessment model.
2   This programme is described in Jessup (1990b) The accreditation of prior learning in the context of NVQs, NCVQ R & D Report No. 7. The full description of the study is contained in a report by Susan Simosko held by the Training Agency and NCVQ.
3   See Newman, J and Llewellin, N (1990) pp. 200–216, The accreditation of prior learning, in Bees, M and Swords, M (1990) for a description of the development at Crosskeys and Newport Colleges.

Chapter 9

1   The motivational advantages of a unit/element structure should not be overlooked; cf Eraut (1989, p. 344):

> Individual elements provide sequenced 'objectives' which should be both relevant and attainable. From the student's point of view, what probably matters most is an objective's position on the immediacy — remoteness continuum (Dressel 1976). Many objectives will appear to students both as conceptually remote, because they are far from what seems to be relevant (...) and be temporally remote because their utility lies far in the future. Perceiving links between their immediate objectives and possible ultimate goals can be crucial for some students' motivation.

2   A description of the system is given in 'Developing a National System of Credit Accumulation and Transfer', NCVQ Information Note No. 1 (1988a).
3   The NCVQ offers a variety of publications which described the National Record of Vocational Achievement. For a basic description see 'An Introduction to the National Record (1990c) and 'The Procedures Guide to the National Record' (1990d).
4   The new National Certificate, a modular provision for Non-Advanced Further Education in Scotland was introduced in August, 1984. It was based on the concept of 40 hour modules. See 'The National Certificate: Catalogue of Modular Descriptors', session 1989–90, Glasgow, SCOT-

VEC (1989). For original details of the system see Scottish Education Department (1983) '16–18's in Scotland: An Action Plan'.
5   NCVQ, R & D No 8: Schools & college based records of achievement and the NROVA by Learners First (1990) provides an analysis of the requirements for a single record of achievement.

Chapter 10

1   For a basic reference to the National Curriculum see DES:'National Curriculum: from policy to practice. 1989.
2   The best description on the philosophy and methodology underlying the National Curriculum is in 'National Curriculum: Task Group on Assessment: A Report.' (1988), DES and Welsh Office. (commonly referred to as the TGAT report). See also 'Education, Culture and the National Curriculum' (1989) by Denis Lawton.

Chapter 11

1   Jessup (1990a) Common learning outcomes: core skills in A/AS levels and NVQs, NCVQ R & D Report No. 6. The report considers the feasibility of specifying and assessing core skills using the NVQ methodology and suggest a potential framework.
2   The proposals were made in a speech by Mr Kenneth Baker on 15 February, 1989 to the annual conference of the Association of Colleges of Further and Higher Education. It was subsequently published by DES under the title: 'Further Education: A New Strategy' (1989).
3   The National Curriculum Council report was entitled 'Core skills 16–19: A Response to the Secretary of State' (1990).
4   'Core Skills in NVQs', NCVQ, July, 1990. The report, in response to the Secretary of State for Education, sets out proposals and a timescale for a programme to create a core skills framework, jointly with the Secondary Education and Assessment Council and other national bodies, and introduce core skills to NVQs.

Chapter 12

1   The CBI report 'Towards a Skills Revolution' (1989) proposes that vocational education and training is targeted on NVQs and NVQ units. It recommends individual action planning, records of achievement and identifies the need for improved guidance. The TUC generally support these proposals, see 'Skills 2000' (1989). The government's Youth Training and

Employment Training schemes have adopted NVQ and units as output targets and a means of designing programmes and the National Record of Vocational Achievement; initial assessment, the accreditation of prior learning and individual action planning is being promoted and the NVQ database is being introduced via TECs.

Chapter 13

1 A recent report from Lancaster University. Saunders, M., Fuller, A., Lobley, D. (1990) 'Emerging Issues in the Utilisation of NVQs', NCVQ R & D Report No 5, provides a salutary reminder of life on the shop floor in many companies. One issue it identified was the effects of peer group pressure (p. 14):

> From the interviewees' perceptions two observations are worth noting. The first concerns the power of peer group pressure to dissuade individuals from appearing too enthusiastic. Being keen to learn or train may be seen as 'sucking up' to the management. It may be important to identify in any particular company context, the extent to which there is a strong sense of group identity amongst operatives which might discipline individuals from 'standing out'. . . .

> 'We have a few problems with "cattyness", some thinking that you are "getting above yourself" wanting to go better that the rest of them. This puts some off doing extra, like training.'
> (Machine Operator, Plastics)

Chapter 14

1 Since writing this chapter a further book has been published 'National Vocational Qualifications and Further Education (1990) by Mike Bees and Madeleine Swords, a collection of papers which adds further experience on the introduction of NVQs to colleges.

Chapter 15

1 See Note 2 to Chapter 10 and reference DES and Welsh Office (1988).
2 Lawton (1989) observes:

> The new national curriculum is likely to transform the role of the teacher, gradually but very significantly. The good teacher

will no longer be just an efficient instructor, but will have to become an expert classroom manager and organiser of learning experiences. (p. 86)

Teachers must also be able to diagnose the problems and diffi-culties of individual pupils, keeping records of them, attempt alternative strategies of teaching, and record successes and failures. Apart from differences in intelligence, which may be related to learning speed, there are other personality differences in learning style which are sometimes ignored by teachers, or only treated at an intuitive level. The professional teacher will be able to categorise individual pupils in a variety of ways and teach accordingly. Thus, teachers need to have a repertoire of teaching styles as well as the ability to diagnose individual differences in learning — including problems of understanding. (p. 87)

Chapter 16

1 See UDACE (1990).
2 Ball, Sir Christopher (1990) 'More Means Different: Widening Access to Higher Education' is the final report of an RSA/Industry Matter project.

Chapter 20

In so far as the process of learning is related to curriculum theory, it is important to appreciate that the outcomes model does not neglect the other essential constituents of a curriculum, which may be listed as teaching and learning, subject matter, and assessment, linked together by aims. The 'out-comes' model is outcome-led — not outcome dominated to the exclusion of everything else. Because all the constituents in a curriculum are essentially related, if one is affected, all are affected. The outcomes model seeks to bring about change by focusing on outcomes referenced against requirements in the world outside education. This external reference provides an anchor point around which other variables may swing,

References

BALL, SIR CHRISTOPHER (1990) 'More means different: widening access to higher education', Final Report, *Industry Matters*, London, RSA.

BALL, S.J. and GOODSON, I. (Eds) (1985) *Teachers' Lives and Careers*, London, Falmer Press.

BECKER, H.S. (1968) *Making the Grade*, Chichester, Wiley.

BECKER, H.S. and GEER, B. (1958) 'The fate of idealism in the medical school', *American Sociological Review*, 23, pp. 50–56.

BECKER, H.S., GEER, B., HUGHES, E.C. and STRAUSS, A.L. (1961) *Boys in White: Student Culture in Medical School: An Interactionalist Viewpoint*, London, Routledge & Kegan Paul.

BEES, M. and SWORDS, M. (1990) *National Vocational Qualifications and Further Education*, London, Kogan Page and NCVQ.

BOREHAM, N.C. (1989) 'Modelling medical decision making under uncertainty', *British Journal of Educational Psychology*, 59, pp. 187–99.

BOREHAM, N.C. (1990) 'An investigation of the methodological issues relating to specifying professional competence', unpublished report to NCVQ.

BLOOM, B.S. (Ed.) (1956) *Taxonomy of Educational Objectives. Handbook 1: Cognitive Domain*, New York, McKay.

BLOOM, B.S. (1971) 'Mastery learning', in BLOCK (Ed.) (1971)

BOBBIT, F. (1918) *The Curriculum*, Boston Mass., Houghton Mifflin.

BRUNER, J.S. (1966) *Towards a Theory of Instruction*, Cambridge, Mass., Harvard University Press.

BURKE, J.W. (1985) 'Concord sixth form college: The possibility of school without conflict', in BALL, S.J. and GOODSON, I. (1985).

BURKE, J.W. (Ed.) (1989a) *Competency Based Education and Training*, London, Falmer Press.

BURKE, J.W. (1989b) 'The implementation of NVQs', pp. 109–31, in Burke (1989a).

BURKE, J. and JESSUP, G. (forthcoming) 'Disentangling validity from reliability', in NUTTALL, D. (Ed.) (forthcoming).

CASSELS, J. (1990) *Britain's Real Skill Shortage and what to do about it*, London, Policy Studies Institute.

COFFMAN, W.E. (1971) 'Essay examinations' in THORNDIKE, R.L. (Ed.) (1971).

COHEN, L. and MANION, L. (1981) *Perspectives on Classrooms and Schools*, London, Holt.

CONFEDERATION OF BRITISH INDUSTRIES (CBI) (1989a) *Towards a Skills Revolution — a Youth Charter*, Interim report of the Vocational Education and Training Task Force, London, CBI.

CBI (1989b) *Towards a Skills Revolution*, Report of the Vocational Education and Training Task Force, London, CBI.

CBI and NCVQ (1990) *National targets and the Implications for NVQ Levels*, London, CBI and NCVQ.

DE and DES (1986) *Working Together: Education and Training*, Cmnd 9823, London, HMSO.

DEPARTMENT OF EDUCATION (1989a) *National Curriculum: From Policy to Practice*, London, HMSO.

DES (1989b) 'Further Education: A new strategy', speech by the Rt. Hon. Kenneth Baker, Secretary of State for Education, to conference of ACFHE, London, HMSO.

DES and DE (1985) *Education and Training for Young People, Cmnd 9482*, London, HMSO.

DES and WELSH OFFICE (1988) *National Curriculum: Task Group on Assessment and Testing [TGAT]: A Report*, London, HMSO.

DEPARTMENT OF EMPLOYMENT (1988) *Employment in the 90s, Cmnd 540*, London, HMSO.

DE (1989) *Training in Britain, Study of Funding Activity and Attitudes*, London, HMSO.

DRESSEL, P.L. (1976) *Handbook of Academic Achievement*, San Francisco, Josey-Bass.

ERAUT, M. (1988) 'What happened to learning design', in H. MATHIAS, N. RUSHBY and R. BUGGET (Eds), *Designing New Systems and Technologies of Learning, Aspects of Educational Technology*, London, Kogan Page.

ERAUT, M. (1989a) 'Specifying and using objectives', in ERAUT (Ed.) (1989b).

ESLAND, G.M. (1971) 'Teaching and learning as the organisation of knowledge', pp. 70–115, in YOUNG, M.F.D.

GOFFMAN, I. (1959) *The Presention of Self in Everyday Life*, reissued by Penguin Books (1969), Harmondsworth, Penguin.

HAFFENDEN, I. and BROWN, A. (1989) 'Towards the implementation of competence based curricula in colleges of FE', pp. 132–70, in BURKE, J. (1989a).

HAMMERSLEY, M. (1977) *Teachers Perspectives*, Open University Educational Studies, A second level course, E 202, Schooling and Society, Units 9 and 10, Block II, The Process of Schooling, Milton Keynes, Open University Press.

HARTOG, P., RHODES, E.C. and BURT, C. (1936) *The marks of Examiners*, London, MacMillan.

HIRST, P.H. (1971) 'What is teaching?' *Journal of Curriculum Studies*, 3.

HOLLY, D. (Ed.) (1974) *Education or Domination*, London, Arrow.

HOLT, J. (1969) *How Children Fail*, Penguin, Harmondsworth.

HOTEL AND CATERING TRAINING BOARD (1987) *Caterbase Guidelines*, London, HCTB.

HUTCHINSON, D. (1990) 'Students with special needs', in BEES and SWORDS (Ed.).

ILLICH, I.D. (1971) *Deschooling Society*, New York, Harper and Row.

INGENKAMP, K. (1977) *Educational Assessment*, Slough, National Foundation for Educational Research.

JESSUP, G. (1983) 'Developing national standards in the YTS core: feasibility of 'Standard Tasks', AGCS paper 83/37', MSC, (unpublished)

JESSUP, G. (1985a) 'Commentary on assessment', p. 40, in Watts A.G.

JESSUP, G. (1985b) *Technical Note on the New Training Initiative: Implications for Standards, Assessment Procedures and Accreditation*, Sheffield, MSC (also reproduced at Appendix 'A').

JESSUP, G. (1989) 'The emerging model of vocational education and training', in BURKE (Ed.) (1989a).

JESSUP, G. (1990a) 'Common learning outcomes: Core skills in A/AS levels and NVQs', *NCVQ R&D Report No. 6*, London, NCVQ.

JESSUP, G. (1990b) 'Accreditation of prior learning in the context of National Vocational Qualifications, *NCVQ R&D Report No. 7*, London, NCVQ.

LABOUR PARTY (1990) *Investing in Britain's Future: Labour's Programme for Post-16 Education and Training*, London, Labour Party.

LACHENMANN, G. (1988) 'Vocational and general education in England', in Rohrs (1988).

LAMMERMAN, H. (1927) 'Das Mannkeimer kombinierte Verfchron der Begabtenanslese Betherft der Zeitschrift fur angewandte', *Psychologie*, 40, p. 197.

LAWTON, D. (1989) *Education, Culture and the National Curriculum*, London, Hodder and Stroughton.

LEARNERS FIRST (1990) *School and College Based Records of Achievement and NROVA, NCVQ R & D Report No. 8*, London, NCVQ.

MAGER, R.F. (1962) *Preparing Instructional Objectives*, Palo Alto, California, Fearon.

MANPOWER SERVICES COMMISION (MSC) (1981) *A New Training Initiative; Agenda for Action*, London, HMSO.

MSC (1984) 'Standards in clerical and administrative occupations: Managing Agents Guide to standard tasks', prepared by the Oxford Group, MSC.

MSC and DES (1986) *Review of Vocational Qualifications in England and Wales*, London, HMSO.

MANSFIELD, B. and MATHEWS, D. (1985) *Job Competence — A Description for use in Vocational Education and Training*, Work based learning project,

Blagdon, Further Education Staff College.

MILLER, C., HOGAN, J., PRINGLE, S. and WEST, G. (1988) *Credit Where Credit is Due*, Glasgow, SCOTVEC.

MITCHELL, L. (1989) 'Occupational standards for dental surgery assistants', *NCVQ R&D Report No. 1*, London, NCVQ.

MITCHELL, L. and CUTHBERT, T. (1989) *Insufficient Evidence, the Final Report of the Competency Testing Project*, Glasgow, SCOTVEC.

NATIONAL COUNCIL FOR VOCATIONAL QUALIFICATIONS (NCVQ) (1989a) *The NVQ Criteria and Related Guidance*, London, NCVQ.

NCVQ (1988b) 'Assessment in National Vocational Qualifications', *NCVQ Information Note No. 4*, London, NCVQ.

NCVQ (1988c) *Access and Equal Opportunities in Relation to National Vocational Qualifications, Information Note 3*, London, NCVQ,

NCVQ (1989b) *Assessment in NVQs: Use of Evidence from Prior Achievement ('APL'), Information Note 5*, London, NCVQ.

NCVQ (1990a) *Establishing the NVQ Framework: Critical Path to 1992*, (unpublished report).

NCVQ (1990b) *NVQ Framework: Progress to Date*, London, NCVQ.

NCVQ (1990c) *An Introduction to the National Record*, London, NCVQ.

NCVQ (1990d) *The Procedures Guide to the National Record*, London, NCVQ.

NCVQ (1990e) 'Core skills in NVQs: Response to the Secretary of State', July, 1990, NCVQ.

NCVQ AND TRAINING AGENCY (TA) (1990) 'Developing NVQs', *National Vocational Qualifications Information and Guidance Notes, No. 1*, London, NCVQ/TA.

NATIONAL CURRICULUM COUNCIL (1990) *Core Skills: 16–19: A Response to the Secretary of State*, York, NCC.

NEAVE, G. (1974) 'The "free schoolers"', in HOLLY, D. (1974) STENHOUSE, L. (1975) *An Introduction to Curriculum Research and Development*, London, Heineman.

NEWMAN, J. and LLEWELLIN, N. (1990) 'The accreditation of prior learning (APL)', in BEES and SWORDS (Ed.) (1990).

OATES, T. (1989) 'Emerging issues: the response of HE to competency based approaches', in BURKE (Ed.) (1989a).

ROHRS, H. (1988) (Ed.) *Vocational and General Education in Western Industrial Societies*, London, Symposium Books.

SAUNDERS, M., FULLER, A. and LOBLEY, D. (1990) *Emerging Issues in the Utilisation of NVQs, R & D Report No. 5*, London, NCVQ.

SCOTTISH EDUCATION DEPARTMENT (1983) *16–18s in Scotland: An Action Plan*, Edinburgh, SED.

SCOTVEC (1989), *The National Certificate: Catalogue of Modular Descriptors, Session 1989–90*, Glasgow, SCOTVEC.

SHACKLETON, JENNY (1989) '*An achievement-led college*', pp. 102–8, in BURKE, J. (1989a).

SIMS, V.M. (1931) 'The objectivity, reliability and validity of an essay examination graded by rating', *Journal of Educational Research*, 24, pp. 216–23.

STARCH, D. and ELLIOT, E.C. (1912) 'Reliability of the grading of high school work in English', *School Review* 21, 254–9.

STENHOUSE, L. (1975) *An Introduction to Curriculum Research and Development*, London, Heinemann.

STONES, E. (1966) *An Introduction to Educational Psychology*, London, Methuen.

TIMES EDUCATIONAL SUPPLEMENT (1990) 'No quick fix for training', 15 June 1990, p. A19.

TRADES UNION CONGRESS (TUC) (1989) *Skills 2000*, London, TUC.

TRAINING AGENCY (TA), DE (1988a) 'The definition of competences and performance criteria, Development of standards for national certification', *Guidance Note No. 3*, Sheffield, TA.

TA, DE, (1988b) 'Issues in assessment. Development of standards for national certification', *Guidance Note No. 5*, Sheffield, TA.

TA, DE (1989) 'Developing standards by reference to functions, Development of standards for national certification', *Guidance Note No. 2*, Sheffield, TA.

TYLER, R.W. (1949) *Basic Principles of Curriculum and Instruction*, Illinois, University of Chicago Press.

TUXWORTH, E. (1989) 'Combetency based education and training: Background and origins', pp. 10–25, in BURKE, J. (1989a).

UDACE (1990) *An Agenda for Access: A Strategy Paper*, Leicester, Unit for the Development of Adult Continuing Education.

VERNEY, A. (1945) 'Underground Story' in The Spectator, 23 February; reissued in GLASS, F. and MARSDEN-SMEDLEY, P. (Eds) (1989) *Articles of War*, London, Grafton.

WATTS, A.G. (Ed.) (1985) *Education and Training 14–18: Policy and Practice*, Cambridge, CRAC.

VERNEY, A. (1945) 'Underground Story' in *The Spectator*, 23rd February; reissued in GLASS, F. and MARSDEN-SMEDLEY, P. (eds) (1989) *Articles of War* Grafton: London.

WEINLEIN, A. (1943) *Pharmacy as a Profession in Wisconsin* unpublished Masters thesis, Department of Sociology, University of Chicago, p. 89, quoted in Goffman (1959), p. 55.

WOOD, R., JOHNSON, C., BLINKHORN, S., ANDERSON, S. and HALL, J. (1988) *Boning, Blanching and Backtacking: Assessing Performance in the Workplace*, St. Albans, Psychometric Research & Development Ltd.

YOUNG, M.F.D. (Ed.) (1971) *Knowledge and Control*, London, Collier-Macmillan.

Appendices

Appendix A

Drafted December 1984
Revised March   1985

Technical Note on the
NEW TRAINING INITIATIVE:
IMPLICATIONS FOR STANDARDS,
ASSESSMENT PROCEDURES AND ACCREDITATION

by Gilbert Jessup, Quality Branch, Manpower Services Commission

'At the heart of the initiative lie standards of a new kind' (MSC, 1981)

Introduction

1   As the starting point it may be useful to review what was actually said on the subject of standards in 'A New Training Initiative: An Agenda for ACTION' (MSC, December, 1981). First objective One:

> we must develop skill training including apprenticeship in such a way as to enable young people entering at different ages and with different educational attainments to acquire agreed standards of skill appropriate to the jobs available and to provide them with a basis for progression through further learning.

Although the initial statement of this objective referred to 'young' people (as above) it is clear from the overall NTI philosophy that the objective was to provide access to training for people of all ages, thus the word 'young' has since been deleted (see 'A New Training Initiative: Modernization of Occupational Training: A Position Statement', MSC, July, 1984)

2   Then in the section headed 'Standards':

At the heart of the initiative lie standards of a new kind. Such standards are essential for the following reasons:

i   modernization of skills training including apprenticeship can only be achieved if we can replace time serving by standards of training achievement and ensure all those who reach such standards, by whatever route and whatever age, are recognized and accepted as competent;

ii if all young people are to have access to basic training, they and employers will want to have a recognized record of skills, knowledge and experience gained and;

iii if there is to be wider access to opportunities for adults, there must be a recognized system which allows the individual to build upon what he has and secure recognition for what he has gained to date.

3   And this section of the report goes on to conclude:

So the standards will need to be:

explicit: so that firms and individuals know what they are and where information about them can be obtained;

agreed: so that there can be no doubt about them and their standing;

widely accessible: to young people and to adults;

flexible: in response to changing, and sometimes different, needs of individuals and localities through a variety of forms of provision (eg education, full-time and part-time training);

progressive: so that people with a 'portfolio' of skills, knowledge and experience can build upon that as they seek to adapt to technological and market changes, to improve their prospects or to explore their potential;

testable: so that they embody an agreed, appropriate and common standard of training achievement which can be certified as such.

4   The report also adds:

. . . we intend to examine for key occupations:

— the tasks which the job actually entails;

— the skills, knowledge and experience which will equip people to perform those tasks;

— the structure and content of training programmes available to enable people to enter the occupation;

— the mechanism for testing the terminal competence of trainees;
— the means by which terminal training achievement is certified and recorded, as well as;
— any gaps which need to be filled.

Accreditation of Work-based Learning

5   Seeing how programmes have developed over the last three years, as a gap to be filled, we should perhaps spell out the specific need to accredit learning in the workplace. This is in recognition of the emphasis now placed on work-based learning in vocational training, particularly in YTS. The point is covered at paragraph 2 (i) above, by the general reference to the recognition of standards achieved 'by whatever route', but this is not made explicit.

Freestanding Standards

6   The requirement that standards should be specified in a form which makes them accessible to all, 'by whatever route' they have acquired their skills, implies that the standards cannot be defined with respect to a particular course or training programme, or a specified period of experience. The standards must be defined in terms of the performance of an individual without reference to the nature or quality of the training provision. Further there should be no requirement that the individual actually received training, in any formal sense, to achieve the standards. This point is particularly important at a time when we are actively promoting 'Open Tech'. All forms of self tuition, distance learning, computer assisted learning, video and audio cassettes, even reading, will play a more important role in vocational learning and updating in the future. There will also be more recognition of learning through experience (see paragraph 5 above).

Criterion-referenced Standards

7   A further implication, not made explicit, but which follows from relating standards to the requirements of jobs and open to all who achieve them, is that the standards should be criterion referenced. In particular they should be referenced against the requirements of jobs. This would point to a change in much of the current practice in accreditation, where performance is judged in relation to the performance of other trainees (norm-referencing).

Comprehensive Coverage of Skill Requirements

8   A technical issue, which is not addressed but which can be reasonably inferred from the NTI philosophy, is the extent to which it is adequate to assess by sampling the skills and knowledge required in jobs (as is common in traditional examinations) or whether a more comprehensive coverage is required. The requirement that the standards should be 'explicit, so that firms and individuals know what they are', implies that the standards must provide a fairly comprehensive coverage of the skills required in jobs otherwise there would be the danger that trainees would only prepare for the standards specified. This does not necessarily rule out the possibility of presenting only a sample in a terminal assessment, provided candidates did not know what sample would be chosen. But in general if we are to move towards more objective statements of what people can actually do we are moving away from assessment by sampling towards comprehensive coverage.

Standards and Assessment Procedures

9   It is worthwhile making a distinction between (a) the specification of a standard and (b) the procedures that might be used to assess the performance of an individual against the standards. These two concepts are very frequently inseparable in formal assessment examination or assessment procedures. For example, if we consider the standards of 'O' level in Physics, the standard could only be inferred from an analysis of the examination procedure. This would need to include an analysis of the questions and the marking procedure. An additional complication would result from the fact that candidates have choice in the questions they answer. It is clear that any statement on the standard of Physics implied by an 'O' level qualification would be extremely complex. But the main point to note is that any concept of standard (as defined by NTI) which exists in respect to such examinations is imbedded in the examination procedure and could only be inferred from it.

10   A similar confusion between concepts of assessment and standard frequently exists in our everyday judgements because assessment often takes place in the absence of specified standards in which case the term 'assessment' refers to both determining the standard (often very roughly and sometimes unconsciously by the assessor) as well as making judgements in respect of it. Assessment invariably embodies some concept of standard even though the assessor may not be aware of the standard he or she is adopting.

11   The majority of problems people associate with assessment are really problems of specifying standards. For example, when different assessors disagree as to whether an employee is competent at his job (as they often

do) they may differ in their assessment of the employee or they may be defining competence (ie the standard for competence) in different ways, or both. To take a simple example, two assessors may disagree in their assessment of competence of a typist because one may be adopting a standard of 30 words per minute while the second may be judging against 50 words per minute. If both first agreed on the same standard (criteria of competence) they would clearly come much closer in their assessments.

12 It should be evident that in the absence of agreed standards it is impossible for different assessors to achieve general agreement in their assessments. That is to say it is impossible to develop reliable and valid assessment procedures in the absence of agreed standards.

13 The more precise we make our specification of standards the more we reduce the scope for interpretation in making assessments and thus the more accurate our assessments should be. On the other hand a too precise specification of the task tends to limit the generality and thus the value of the assessment. Some compromise between these conflicting aims must be achieved.

The Specification of Standards

14 The formulation of standards of the kind we are considering has two components. First, it is necessary to specify with some precision the activity, task or skill with which we are concerned. This will normally include the conditions under which the activity/task should be performed. Second, it is necessary to specify the criteria by which success will be judged. It is assumed that the assessment to be made is to standards achieved (can do) or not achieved. The task description and criteria of success form a package. Considerations such as time and accuracy of performance can be built into the task description (eg 5 minutes allowed) or into the criteria of success (eg task must have been completed within 5 minutes).

Level of Aggregation of Activity at which Standards are Set

15 In education and training it has been the tradition to specify standards and accredit achievement in relation to large blocks of achievement such as a course or training programme lasting perhaps several years (eg GCE 'O' levels, apprenticeships, university degrees). If we are to meet the NTI criteria, we shall need to specify standards at the level of skills and tasks, relatively small units of activity, in relation to the overall requirement for competence in an occupation. This stems from the need to stipulate the activity with some degree of precision (paragraph 14

above). It also follows from the requirement to accredit what people 'can do' and the presentation of 'a portfolio of skills'.

16 Apart from technical necessity, the specification of standards and accreditation of relatively small units of activity has several advantages.

(a) trainees can be accredited with the skills they have achieved (to standard) even if they have not achieved all the learning objectives in the training programme. (In many existing programme) one has nothing to show at the end unless one gains the full qualification),

(b) the standards provide a series of goals for trainees to aim at as they progress through a programme which aids motivation and learning,

(c) it provides much greater flexibility (see modular structure below)

Continuous Assessment

17 Although specifying standards in relation to small units of activity does not preclude terminal assessment and accreditation (ie a demonstration of all skills and knowledge at the end of the programme) it lends itself more naturally to some form of continuous assessment. That is to say assessments are made and recorded at the stage of the programme when the skills and knowledge are acquired. This has several advantages:

(a) it allows trainees to progress at their own speed (provided the system of training can cope with this)

(b) continuous assessment both motivates and informs the learning process; that is to say it serves a 'formative' function in addition to the summative accreditation function with which this paper is concerned,

(c) it allows for the accreditation of what has been achieved even when trainees leave before completing the programme of training.

The advantages of continuous assessment overlap and follow from those of accrediting relatively small units of activity (paragraph 16) which makes continuous summative assessment possible.

A Modular Structure for Accreditation and Training

18 One administrative disadvantage of assessing at the level of tasks or skills is that it generates a large volume of information. For a variety of purposes some form of summary is required. The New Training Initiative does not specifically refer to a modular structure for accreditation and training but the criteria specified lead naturally in that direction. A

module may be defined as a group of related skills and knowledge which forms a recognizable block of activity within an occupation or a subject. The 16+ Action Plan in Scotland provides a model of what a modular system might look like. In Scotland the size of the modules is based upon the notional concept of 40 hours of education or training. But more specifically the modules are defined in terms of their standards (described as learning objectives).

19 In a modular system of accreditation and training there are clearly advantages in having modules of approximately the same size. The size adopted would be the same compromise between very small units to maximise on the opportunities for accreditation and to achieve flexibility and larger units for administrative convenience (ie to avoid unwieldy numbers modules). A system built around the concept of somewhere between 2 to 6 weeks of training (ie the standards that could be achieved in that time by the average trainee) probably represents a fair compromise.

20 A modular system of accreditation has considerable advantages in allowing rapid adaptation to changing occupational requirements due to technological or other changes. It is easier to change, update or delete a relatively small module than adapt a lengthy syllabus. It further allows much greater flexibility in the classification and re-classification of occupational requirements as the structure of our industries change.

Alternative Assessment Procedures

21 Although the advantages of continuous assessment running throughout a training programme have been spelled out above, if this is the only way in which the standards can be accredited it ties accreditation to a training programme and contravenes one of the requirements of NTI. We thus wish to develop assessment procedures which can deliver assessment to standards (and accreditation) either during a formal training programme, during a work-based training programme (ie in the workplace) or separate from either (eg a 'testing centre'). The advantage of defining standards as described above is that they stand alone, independent of programmes of training. We thus need to develop alternative assessment procedures that can be used to accredit achievement to the same standards in different contexts and locations.

HOW DO EXISTING PRACTICES MEET THE REQUIREMNETS?

There are very few examples of existing education or training standards and associated accreditation systems which meet the criteria specified by NTI in all respects. The driving test provides us with a useful model with which we are all familiar. It is a skills test with an additional knowledge requirement (the Highway Code). It is criterion-referenced. The test is open to everyone irrespective of how they acquired their skills and knowledge. It does not allow for continuous assessment or part accreditation but it is a relatively small unit of skilled activity and may be regarded as a module of training/accreditation within the above framework.

Skills Tests

23 Skills tests of the type developed by the City and Guilds London Institute and some Industrial Training Boards offer examples of what is possible in the accreditation of occupational skills. The typing exams accredited by the Royal Society of Arts offer another example. So far the application of skills tests has tended to concentrate on specific skills within certain occupations, often within specific companies, rather than comprehensive coverage of the skill and knowledge requirements of an occupation (the concept of occupational competence). Skills tests are normally provided only at certain test centres, often company test centres, and linked to certain programmes of training.

24 To expand the concept of skills tests to meet the requirements of NTI and to provide a cost-effective means of accreditation, a number of developments would be needed. First, the range of skills tests available would need to cover a range of skills within a job or occupation. Second, the skills tests (or standards associated with them) need to be brought into and delivered as part of a process of continuous assessment during training programmes in training institutions or in the workplace. There are many skills or activities in the workplace which can readily or sensibly be assessed outside that context. There are also strong economic reasons for making assessments at the place of learning. Third, the tests would need to be built into a comprehensive modular structure of accreditation and training.

Standard Tasks

25 An alternative approach being developed by the MSC and Oxford Group, to meet the NTI criteria, is built round the concept of 'standard tasks'. The approach has a good deal in common with skills tests but starts with the formulation of standards for tasks performed in the workplace without adherence to any particular method of assessment. Standard tasks could in many cases be delivered in the form of skills tests and offered as free-standing examinations although it is not anticipated that this will be the most common form of delivery.

26 The methodology behind this approach starts with an analysis of an occupation or occupational area and the identification and classification of the tasks performed in jobs within that category (as proposed in the

NTI report, para 4 above). Agreement is reached on the specification of the tasks and the criteria by which success is commonly judged is derived by consensus through supervisors and employers. The standard tasks thus derived can be projects or assignments, and used as bench-marks against which to make assessments.

27 Through these various methods of assessing to standards, particularly the scope offered for local assessment by supervisors in the workplace and tutors in colleges, standard tasks offer the potential for the cost effective means of realizing the new kinds of standards required by NTI. The approach still needs considerable refinement but the results of de-velopment work to date in the context of the Youth Training Scheme are encouraging (see Standards in Clerical and Administrative Occupa-tions, MSC, 1984 also Standards in Retail Occupations, MSC, 1984 and associated guidance).

28 The intention is that standard tasks should be grouped into modules for accreditation and training.

Conclusion

29 The criteria for specifying standards and developing accreditation sys-tems as stated in the New Training Initiative are stringent. Few current practices meet the requirement. The approaches offered by skills testing and the formulation of standard tasks with associated assessment pro-cedures would appear to point the way forward.

Appendix B

Executive Summary and Targets set in 'Towards a Skills Revolution', CBI, 1989; Report of the Vocational Education and Training Task Force.

EXECUTIVE SUMMARY

Britain's skills levels are lower than those in most of its competitor countries and the gap is widening. Despite annual employer expenditure on training of over £18 billion and important initiatives in the education field, a quantum leap is needed in Britain's education and training performance.

To maintain and improve Britain's position in an increasingly competitive world nothing short of a skills revolution is required. Action is urgently needed.

This report sets out the Task Force's programme of action for bridging the skills gap. It is concerned with investment in people — first and foremost the foundation skills of young people and secondly, the needs of the 80 percent of the year 2000 workforce who are already in employment.

Individuals are now the only source of sustainable competitive advantage. Efforts must be focused on mobilizing their commitment and encouraging self-development and lifetime learning.

Yet skill needs can only be met by the creation of effective training markets in which the customers — individuals and their employers — exercise more influence over education and training provision. Employers must be persuaded to manage their skill needs like any other business challenge, through systematic investment in training.

Government also has a central role to play. It must offer the nation a coherent vocational education and training policy, especially for young people. Exchequer funding must be available to provide the foundation skills which the nation requires.

The Task Force's recommendations address each of these needs.

World class targets are set for the nation's skills revolution. The practice of employing 16–18 year olds without training leading to nationally recognized qualifications must stop. These national attainment targets (in Chapter One) would make qualifications at craftsman, technician and their equivalent levels in service industries the norm. They also seek to make lifetime learning a reality throughout the workforce.

Secondly, Britain must put individuals first and provide opportunities whereby everyone can make maximum use of their potential. Chapter Two describes 'Careership' proposals which bridge the divide between education and training for the first time and are just as valid for the more academic as they are for the more vocational. They give young people the opportunity to manage their own careers. This can be achieved by:

- introducing personal profiles with the necessary professional careers advice and support
- providing each 16 year old with a cash credit to give them real buying power in the education and training market
- offering more relevant transferable skills and broad based qualifications.

Thirdly, all employers must become Investors in Training. Chapter Three sets out the experience of those employers who have been most effective in managing their skills needs. They treat training as an investment which must be systematically planned and evaluated.

Finally, a real market must be created for training. Chapter Four describes how the introduction of individual credits would bring this about. Government should fund the learning costs of courses for young people leading to nationally recognized qualifications. Employers should offer jobs and meet the wage costs of young people. At a time when the numbers of young people are falling these moves would replace the choice between a job or training by a job and training.

The new Training and Enterprise Councils would have a key role as regulators of the local training market — ensuring that employers meet their obligations, and that providers are responsive to current needs and demands while preparing for the future. It is crucial that they have a broad, strategic remit.

The Task Force is issuing this report in response to growing employer concerns that the skills gap can no longer be ignored. The economic and social costs of doing so are unacceptable. A revolution in expectations, standards and the delivery of education and training must take place.

TARGETS AND ACTION

The Task Force believes that it is necessary to set world class targets for the progress which should be made during the period of foundation learning. These should be:

- immediate moves to ensure that by 1995 almost all young people attain NVQ Level II or its academic equivalent (ie 5 GSCEs at A–C grade)
- all young people should be given an entitlement to structured training, work experience or education leading to NVQ Level III or its academic equivalent (ie 2 'A' levels and 5 GSCEs at A–C grade)
- by the year 2000 half of the age group should attain NVQ Level III or its academic equivalent
- all education and training provision should be structured and designed to develop self-reliance, flexibility and broad competencies as well as specific skills.

Paragraph 23

Further targets for company and adult training should be established alongside those for young people:

- by 1995, all employees should take part in company-driven training or developmental activities as the norm
- by 1995, at least half of the employed workforce should be aiming for updated or new qualifications within the NVQ framework, preferably in the context of individual action plans and with support from employers
- by the year 2000, 50 percent of the employed workforce should be qualified to NVQ Level III or its academic equivalent as a minimum
- by 1995, at least half of medium sized and larger companies should qualify as 'Investors in Training' as assessed by the relevant Training and Enterprise Council.

Paragraph 25

Action is needed in four areas:

- motivating people to learn within a coherent education and training framework
- creating an individual focus through personal profiles
- giving individuals real buying power in a new education and training market
- offering transferable skills and relevant qualifications

Paragraph 29

Careership should provide a single framework to guide and structure the development of foundation skills from 14 to 18 and a basis for continuous learning and training throughout working life.

Paragraph 33

A successful vocational education and training system should be built on the local delivery of national standards. There should be a funding partnership between employers, employees and the Exchequer.

Paragraph 106

Recommendations addressed principally at Government

Implementing the following recommendations can be afforded within existing levels of public expenditure, as employers would pay the wage costs of young people under the partnership this report proposes, thus releasing significant sums now spent via YTS on income support to pay for training.

One national system of records of achievement and action plans should be used both in schools and employment, pre-16 and post-16.

Paragraph 39

A major review should be undertaken to clarify the role, responsibility, funding requirements and relationships of the major careers guidance agencies.

Paragraph 45

Government should fund a credit for all 16 year olds to meet the learning costs associated with courses leading to NVQ Level III or its academic equivalent (A levels).

Paragraph 47

Consideration should be given to introducing a personal income tax allowance of, say £1000 per annum for anyone working towards a nationally recognized qualification in their own time, where a credit is not also being used.

Paragraph 53

YTS has a valuable role to play as one of the elements in a broader Careership framework, especially in continuing to promote equal opportunities and providing help for those with special needs through adequate resourcing of premium provision.

Paragraphs 59 & 119

Employment Training:

- must take even more account of the varying training needs of the client group
- needs to reflect an enhanced role for the training managers who will

need to be specialized intermediary agencies responsible for action planning.

Exhibit 16

The Task Force supports the Government proposal to put the remaining statutory Industrial Training Boards on a voluntary basis, but special considerations apply to the construction industry and the construction sector of the engineering industry.

Paragraph 109

A nationwide discretionary maintenance allowance is recommended for those denied educational opportunity through poverty, and for those who are genuinely unable to find an employer training place.

Paragraph 120

Dealing with the shortage of teachers will require some combination of:

- changes to the pay and reward structure
- ensuring that all teachers meet the required quality standards
- closing under-utilized schools
- improving links between schools and local businesses.

Paragraph 132

The Task Force supports Professor Higginson's recommendations for reforming 'A' levels through studying a larger number of subjects and increasing skills-based content.

Exhibit 12

The Training Agency should publish a framework explaining how TECs, Industry Training Organizations and national bodies such as itself will complement each other.

Paragraph 143

As well as modifying TEC design in certain respects (see below), a number of TECs should be used as pilots for the Task Force recommendations, particularly those relating to the use of credits.

Paragraph 150

Recommendations to employers

Any under 18 employment not involving structured education and training leading to recognized qualifications should be eliminated.

Paragraph 22

All employees must become Investors in Training. Investors in Training hold the key to good training practice, through their:

- vision
- business planning
- training objectives and training plans
- training targets
- resourcing and accounting for training
- clear responsibilities for training
- support for self development
- training infrastructure
- evaluation of training
- external focus

Paragraphs 81 to 97

All employers should adopt a common definition of training activity and report on training activity to managers, employees, investors and share-holders.

Paragraph 88

An Investor in Training will link into Careership by providing:

- opportunities to pursue national vocational qualification for young people using their credits
- regularly revised Individual Action Plans
- access to independent careers guidance where necessary.

Paragraph 92

The key to credits as proposed by this report is that the Exchequer contribution should only be available for the off-the-job learning costs, and that the employer would normally offer a job and pay a market wage to the trainee.

Paragraph 113

Employers and colleges will need to work together even more closely in the future.

Paragraph 131

Recommendations relevant to educational and professional interests

Top quality independent careers advice and guidance focused on the individual must be available throughout working life.

Paragraph 45

Careers advisers, Local Education Authorities and training providers and employers should play a greater part in publicising Career Development Loans.

Paragraph 55

In implementing the National Curriculum:

- Greater prominence should be given to cross-curricular themes such as economic awareness and careers education within the curriculum
- There should be an appropriate balance of knowledge and skills within individual subject at school.

Exhibit 12

The outcomes from all training and vocational education should include the following Common Learning Outcomes as core elements:

- values and integrity
- effective communication
- application of numeracy
- applications of technology
- understanding of work and the world
- personal and interpersonal skills
- problem solving
- positive attitudes to change

Paragraph 60

In fulfilling its aims NCVQ needs to make consistent progress in promoting broad based competence.

- NCVQ should press ahead with the development of 'generic' competences to broaden NVQs and to contribute to a national consensus on Common Leaning Outcomes.
- Higher priority should be given to establishing a critical mass of fully accredited qualifications.
- More strenuous efforts at marketing and raising the status of NVQs are required.
- Employer representation on the National Council should be strengthened.
- The use of terms such as diploma, baccalaureat and associate degreeship to which all qualifications would count would help to bridge the education and training divide.
- In order to achieve the above objectives both NCVQ and standards setting work need more resources.

Paragraphs 64 & 67

Investment analysts and financial institutions should give particular attention to the proposed reports by companies on their training activities.

Paragraph 88

The banks' small business advisory services should highlight the importance of training as a core function.

Paragraph 100

Colleges should continue to develop staffing, reward and marketing strategies to meet market demand.

Paragraph 131

Recommendations concerning TECs

The role of TECs must be strategic and they should act as regulators of the training market, rather than as providers of training.

Paragraph 136

TECs should have an overview of all local programmes that relate to vocational education and training.

Paragraph 140

TECs should have sizeable discretionary budgets and extensive scope to adapt national programmes to meet local needs (but within laid down national standards).

Paragraph 141

There is scope for the adoption of a single set of standards by all databases (dealing with information on job, education and training opportunities).

Paragraph 146

In the implementation of Careership, TECs have an important role as regulators of the local training market.

Paragraph 148

TECs should be seeking to continue the skills revolution throughout working life by encouraging 'Investors in Training' and promoting self development.

Paragraph 149

Appendix C

NVQ FRAMEWORK
A PROPOSED SYSTEM OF CLASSIFICATION OF NVQs
BY AREAS OF COMPETENCE

NOTE FOR INFORMAL CONSULTATIONS

Introduction

The complex issue of the most appropriate form of classification to adopt for the horizontal axis of the NVQ framework has been a matter of debate and research since the framework was conceived. It was recognized at an early stage existing classification systems, based upon occupations, industries or training categories, would not be suitable to indicate to users the potential progression routes for the development of competence. One of the primary objectives of the framework is to indicate progression routes which transcend traditional occupational and industry boundaries which currently inhibit employment mobility and career progression.

What is needed is a classification system based upon competence. That is to say a system which groups together those qualifications which are similar in respect of the competences they incorporate. Progression and transfer in employment will be most effective if new jobs build upon the competences practised in previous jobs.

Various forms of analysis have taken place to develop such a classification system. Skill-based and task-based classifications have been explored, but tasks and skills do not adequately describe the broader concept of competence upon which NVQs are based. More recent approaches of the functional analysis of industrial and organizational activity come closer to what is needed.

182

Proposed Functional Classification

The system now proposed derives primarily from analysis by functions. But function does not provide a complete explanation of competence either, as the dimensions of skill and knowledge must also be taken into account. In addition, the current standards development programme derives from a complex network of industry-based bodies, occupational and professional bodies and consortia. This has shaped the structure and groupings of NVQs which have been, and are being, developed. These must also be accommodated in the framework.

The proposed framework, when refined, is considered to represent the best that can be currently produced. It groups together and relates common areas of competence in so far as these can be identified, given our current understanding of competence and its transferability. It accommodates existing NVQs and those under development. Although it does not reflect traditional industrial and occupational groupings, it is hoped that the form of classification will be understood and acceptable to those in industry, and other users.

The proposed classification still needs considerable development and refinement within the sub-functions and at levels below. These can now be developed in association with those in the relevant industrial sectors and occupational areas, within the parameters set to date. Further refinement will also take place as more subsets of standards and NVQs are created. NCVQ will promote a process of rationalization of common competences across sectors and occupations, largely through common units, which will also have implications for the detailed categorization of NVQs.

Functional Labels

It will be seen that the functional language of competence had been adopted throughout to describe the categories. This means adopting the gerund or present participle derived from the verb (a word ending in 'ing') in each category. This is common practice in some occupation areas (eg engineering, farming), while others refer to industrial sectors and the professions tend to refer to subjects or disciplines (e.g. law, medicine). In the latter case one can refer to the function or activity as 'practising law'. It is considered important to retain this principle for consistency and to constantly remind users that the NVQ framework is concerned with competence — the performance of individuals — and not sectors of industry, jobs, subjects or disciplines. Individuals can perform the same function in many different jobs or industries. Drawing attention to such common functions, to facilitate transfer of skills, is one of the primary objectives of the framework.

It is proposed to divide the NVQ framework into twelve major functional categories, each of which is divided into a variable number of sub-functions and further divided into functions at a third level of analysis which corresponds in the current representation of the framework to a column (See NCVQ Report 'The NCVQ Framework' of January 1990). At the third level of analysis we shall have a category which will frequently correspond to the title of an NVQ. Such a title may be common to NVQs at different levels within the same column. In some areas this may still be too general in which case the NVQ titles may correspond to a fourth level of analysis. Occasionally a range of NVQs derive their title from the sub-functions at the second level of analysis and thus span a number of columns (eg Business Adminis-tration, Retail Distribution). It has recently been suggested that the develop-ment of such NVQs, covering a wider area of competence, should be encouraged to ensure that broader based or foundation NVQs are included in the framework.

NVQ Titles

The implication of the above is that we should encourage lead and awarding bodies to adopt functional titles which will locate their position within the NVQ framework. NVQ titles should derive from the category title to which the NVQ is allocated.

NVQ Unit Classification

Because NVQs relate to employment requirements they will often cover a number of different functions. This implies that any form of functional classification applied to NVQs cannot be precise. The NVQ title should refer to the predominant functional area to which the competences relate.

NVQ units on the other hand are smaller and functionally more homogeneous. They will normally relate to a single function. It means that we have the opportunity to develop a more rigorous classification system for units than is possible for NVQs. This is the intention and research will continue on this issue as more units are derived. The unit classification system can be used within the NVQ database to help users make connections between units in different occupational areas and different NVQs. It need not feature explicitly in the presentation of the NVQ framework. It does have implications for unit titles though which should be precise functional specifications of the competence covered.

'Generic' Qualifications and Units

It is proposed that generic qualifications and generic units will be shown in a third dimension of the framework, yet to be developed. Generic qualifications and units will, by definition, be relevant to a wide range of NVQs in the different categories competence in the framework proposed in this paper. It is expected that generic units, when available, will be incorporated in a wide range of NVQs.

Feedback Required

NCVQ would welcome feedback from lead bodies, awarding bodies and other interested users on the proposed form or classification for the NVQ framework.

Detailed proposals on how the analysis of specific functions and sub-functions might be improved would also be welcome.

Further analysis to fill gaps is also required from the relevant sectors and occupations.

Need for Working Framework

It is envisaged that the framework will be refined and improved over a period of time, especially in the finer details of analysis. It can only sensibly evolve through such an iterative process, through consultation and experience. NCVQ and the Training Agency nevertheless urgently need a 'working' framework to structure the development of standards and the creation of NVQs. The proposed framework will be used for this purpose, although planning will be adjusted to take into account changes in the framework as the programme develops.

NVQ Database

We have been able to launch the NVQ database, in which all qualifications and units are currently classified in four ways (SOC, SIC, TOC and Super-class) as well as being accessible by title, without the NVQ classification system being fully in place. The NVQ Framework classification will, when sufficiently developed, become the primary structure to organize and access NVQs and standards in the database.

Gilbert Jessup
Director of Research, Development and Information
2 May 1990

Draft September 1990

NVQ FRAMEWORK
CLASSIFICATION BY AREAS OF COMPETENCE

1 TENDING ANIMALS, PLANTS AND LAND
   1.1 FARMING
      1.1.1 Growing Crops
      1.1.2 Practising Forestry
      1.1.3 Tending Farm Animals
      1.1.4 Fish Farming
   1.2 LANDSCAPING AND GARDENING
      1.2.1 Planting and Growing
      1.2.2 Landscaping
   1.3 CARING FOR ANIMALS
      1.3.1 Breeding Animals
      1.3.2 Caring for Animals
      1.3.3 Training Animals

2 EXTRACTING NATURAL RESOURCES
   2.1 MINING
      2.1.1 Extracting Operations
      2.1.2 Mining Engineering
   2.2 QUARRYING
      2.2.1 Producing
      2.2.2 Excavating
   2.3 EXPLORING AND PRODUCING (GAS AND OIL)
      2.3.1 Exploring
      2.3.2 Drilling
      2.3.3 Producing
   2.4 PROVIDING ENERGY AND WATER
      2.4.1 Maintaining Electricity Supplies
      2.4.2 Processing Water Supplies
      2.4.3 Maintaining Gas Supplies

3 CONSTRUCTING BUILDINGS, HIGHWAYS AND RELATED STRUCTURES
   3.1 CONSTRUCTING
      3.1.1 Concreting
      3.1.2 Bricklaying
      3.1.3 Joining & Carpentry
      3.1.4 Roofing
      3.1.5 Asphalting
      3.1.6 Conserving Buildings

Appendix D

THE CONCEPT OF RELIABILITY IN THE ASSESSMENT OF NVQs

Note by Gilbert Jessup, NCVQ
3 December 1989

Reliability and Validity

It has become common place to quote the concepts of 'reliability and validity' as essential requirements of any assessment system. They almost invariably appear linked together in one phrase as if inseparable. They have become a cliche, and like most cliches are accepted without further thought. This note is to make you think!

As these characteristics of an assessment system are seldom actually measured in qualifications, whether they reach satisfactory levels in any assessment process is a matter of judgement or trust. But the main point I wish to make in this note is that 'reliability' and 'validity' are separate although related concepts. Further, their significance is quite different in the standards-based, criterion-referenced model of assessment which applies to NVQs.

What I am proposing is that we should just forget reliability altogether and concentrate on validity, which is ultimately all that matters.

Reliability

'Reliability' is concerned with the consistency of assessments. One index of reliability can be obtained by comparing the judgements made by an assessor on different occasions when presented with the same evidence. A second index of reliability compares the judgements of different assessors when presented with the same evidence. A third index compares different assessment instruments purportedly attempting to assess the same thing, or sometimes separate components of the same instrument.

Reliability has been given great prominence in norm-referenced systems of assessment because, by definition, the assessment is about comparing individuals with each other. Less emphasis is given to what is actually being measured. What is important is that it should be for all individuals. If everybody does the same thing it is regarded as 'fair' or at least equally unfair.

Typically, in such norm-referenced systems, which have tended to prevail in educational assessment, there is seldom any attempt to relate the assessment to any external criterion. In fact there is often a lack of clarity as to what the objectives of the assessment are, except to discriminate between individuals in some way.

Validity

Validity is concerned with the extent to which an assessment instrument or method actually measures what it is designed to measure. It implies comparison between the assessments and some external criterion, i.e. that which one is trying to access. Within the NVQ model of assessment one clearly has an external reference point for assessment — the statement of competence. In fact the external reference point is defined first, before the method of assessment. Thus one starts by quite explicitly stating the competences required by individuals which then provide the specification for assessment as well as training.

Assuming the statement of competence, through the elements of competence and their performance criteria, correctly sets out what is required, the validity of assessments then becomes a matter of comparing the judgements made on the evidence of competence collected, against the elements of competence.

The sole objective of assessment within the NVQ model, within cost and resource limits, should be to maximise its validity. Reliability as described above is only important in so far as it contributes to this end. In fact, to try to maximise reliability as such might actually reduce validity.

Take an example. If I faithfully observe the performance criteria and make a valid assessment of an individual's competence and you do not, a comparison between us would indicate that the assessment is unreliable. The solution to this problem is not to try and obtain agreement between the two assessments as this would very likely reduce the validity of my assessment. The solution to this problem, and I suggest all similar problems, is to check whether the assessments conform to the requirements in the elements of competence and their performance criteria, ie check the validity. In all circumstances assessment should be checked against the external criterion and not with each other. If two assessments are both valid they will naturally be comparable and thus reliable, but this is incidental.

This issue is of further importance in the NVQ assessment model because different assessors in different contexts may draw upon different sources of evidence in making their assessment of the same element. It is difficult to see in what sense their judgements might be consistent and reliable in such circumstances. What is important is that they both obtain sufficient relevant evidence to attest to competence in respect of the element.

Fairness

I would also suggest that the concept of 'fairness' has changed. I do not see it is necessarily fair if you are incorrectly assessed, or judged on irrelevant information, that I should be also. Fairness is achieved when people who are competent, in that they can meet the performance criteria specified, are assessed as competent, and those who have not yet reached the standard are not assessed as competent. One's appeal to fairness should be judged against the independent specification of competence which is open for all to see.

I can think of no circumstance in which a comparison between assessments would be a better check of the system than comparison between the assessments and the statement of competence. I therefore suggest we drop the concept of reliability in the NVQ model of assessment and concentrate our energies on maximising validity.

Reliability is yet another part of the baggage people carry with them from traditional norm-reference models of assessment.

Index